The Meaning of Life

The Meaning of Life

S. L. Frank

Translated by
Boris Jakim

William B. Eerdmans Publishing Company
Grand Rapids, Michigan / Cambridge, U.K.

Originally published in Russian
under the title *Smysl zhizni*
(published privately, Paris, 1925)

Published 2010 by
Wm. B. Eerdmans Publishing Co.
2140 Oak Industrial Drive N.E., Grand Rapids, Michigan 49505 /
P.O. Box 163, Cambridge CB3 9PU U.K.

Printed in the United States of America

16 15 14 13 12 11 10   7 6 5 4 3 2 1

Library of Congress Cataloging-in-Publication Data

Frank, S. L. (Semen Liudvigovich), 1877-1950.
The meaning of life / S. L. Frank; translated by Boris Jakim.
p.   cm.
ISBN 978-0-8028-6527-4 (pbk.: alk. paper)
1. Life — Religious aspects — Christianity.
2. Meaning (Philosophy) — Religious aspects — Christianity.
I. Title.

BV4509.5.F73   2010
197 — dc22

2010013886

www.eerdmans.com

Contents

Translator's Foreword

S. L. Frank tells us a few simple things. He tells us that, if we do not possess the meaning of life, we are like drowning men who have no way to get to shore. On the other hand, if we do find the meaning of life, we have a means to save ourselves and get to solid ground. The paramount task of our era is to overcome the meaninglessness of life. To remain in this meaninglessness is to die; to find meaning is to be reborn and to live. But what is the meaning of life? How does one define it and how does one find it?

Frank's inquiry into the meaning of life has two aspects, a sociopolitical one and a metaphysical one, and in the end the two aspects are fused into one: Frank explains how all of human life — personal, cosmic, social — can and should be illuminated with meaning. He explores the meanings of the concept "the meaning of life," immersing himself deeper and deeper into spiritual being, until he reaches what he calls the true meaning of life, and this meaning is metaphysical or religious — it is the place where man's soul touches Divinity. And it is Divinity that illuminates life with meaning.

2

S. L. Frank (1877-1950) was one of the leading Russian philosophers of the twentieth century; some authorities consider him to be the most outstanding Russian philosopher of any age. His active philosophical career spanned the half-century from 1902 to 1950; over the course of this period he produced seven book-length treatises on philosophy, as well as several long philosophical essays (of which *The Meaning of Life*, first published in 1925, is one), in addition to a mass of articles and reviews. As will become clear to the reader of *The Meaning of Life*, "Frank held," as a leading Frank scholar, Philip Swoboda, points out, "extremely generous views concerning both the proper scope of philosophy, and the capacity of the philosophical intelligence to illuminate the deepest and most obscure problems of being and human life. He conceived the philosopher as the expounder of an 'integral world-view,' a complete, systematic, and rationally-grounded metaphysical understanding of the cosmos and of man's place in it."[1]

Semyon Liudvigovich Frank was born in 1877 in Moscow.[2] His father, a physician, moved to Moscow from western Russia during the Polish rebellion of 1863. After his father's death in 1882, Frank and Frank's mother went to live with her father, M. M. Rossianski, one of the founders of the Moscow Jewish community in the 1860s. Frank's first teacher was his grandfather, who forced the boy to learn Hebrew and to read the Bible in the original. He would take Frank to the synagogue, where the boy received his first religious impressions, retaining them his entire life. Frank always considered that his Christianity rested on an Old Testament foundation, as the natural development of the religious life of his childhood. There was one other major influence on Frank during his early youth: his father-in-law, V. I. Zak, who had passed his youth in an envi-

---

1. See Swoboda's foreword to S. L. Frank, *Man's Soul: An Introductory Essay in Philosophical Psychology*, trans. Boris Jakim (Athens: Ohio University Press, 1993), p. xii.

2. The biographical data given here are taken from the article written by Victor Frank (S. L. Frank's son), "Semyon Liudvigovich Frank 1877-1950," for the *Sbornik pamiati Semyona Liudvigovich Franka (A Collection of Essays in Memory of Semyon Liudvigovich Frank)*, published in Munich in 1954. Also taken from this article are the quoted excerpts from S. L. Frank's journal.

ronment of revolutionary populism. Zak introduced Frank to the ideological world of Russian socialism and political radicalism. Frank later noted that these ideas had only a superficial influence on him; what truly influenced him was the general atmosphere of ideological seeking, which reinforced the necessity of having a "worldview."

In 1892, Frank's family moved to Nizhnii-Novogorod. As an upper classman at the gymnasium there, Frank joined a Marxist study group and became involved with a group of radical intelligentsia. He was still under the influence of this atmosphere when he enrolled in the Law Faculty of Moscow University as a seventeen-year-old in 1894. He became a member then of the newly formed Social Democrats (the forerunners of the Bolsheviks). In 1896, at the age of nineteen, he broke with his fellow conspirators and renounced radical political activity. He could not tolerate the categorical judgments and the shallowness and ignorance of his "comrades," and he became indifferent to the revolution and practical revolutionary action. While remaining a socialist, Frank began a serious study of political economy, which led him to understand the shakiness and inconsistency of Marx's economic theory.

Student disturbances took place at most Russian universities during the spring of 1899. Although Frank did not actively participate in them, he composed a proclamation, and for that he was arrested and exiled for two years without the right to live in university cities. In the autumn of 1899, he left for Berlin, where he listened to lectures in political economy and philosophy at the university. In Berlin he also wrote his first book: *Marx's Theory of Value and Its Significance*.

Frank returned to Russia in 1901 to resume his studies, and he earned a degree from the University of Kazan. The year 1901 marked the awakening of Frank's philosophical thought. In the winter of 1901-1902 he read Nietzsche's *Also Sprach Zarathustra*. Here is what Frank wrote in his journal concerning the influence of this work:

> From this moment I felt the reality of the spirit, the reality of the depths of my own soul; and without any specific decisions, my inner fate was defined. I became an "idealist," not in the Kantian sense but an idealist-metaphysician, a bearer of a certain spiritual experience, which gave access to the invisible inner reality of being.

For Frank the first decade of the twentieth century became what he called his *Lehr- und Wanderjahre.* He supported himself by translating German philosophical works, and he participated in a number of politico-cultural journals founded by his close friend, the economist P. B. Struve, former leader of the Social Democrats. In 1909 Frank was one of the participants in the celebrated compilation *Landmarks (Vekhi).* In this volume, seven leading philosophers[3] united to criticize the radical worldview of the intelligentsia. We read in Frank's journal:

> *Landmarks* expressed . . . [a] . . . spiritual-social tendency . . . composed of two fundamental themes: the assertion — against the reigning positivism and materialism of the intelligentsia — of the necessity of a religio-metaphysically grounded world-view; and, on the other hand, an acute principled critique of the revolutionary maximalistic strivings of the Russian radical intelligentsia.

Landmarks caused a furor; the volume was received as a brazen betrayal of the sacred tradition of the radical intelligentsia, but it was not without influence on a select minority of the intelligentsia. This influence could be seen in the opposition of a large part of the intelligentsia to the Bolshevik revolution and in the religious repentance and rebirth experienced by many Russian intellectuals after the revolution.

In 1911-12, Frank passed his master's examination, and in the fall of 1912 he became a lecturer at Petersburg University. He converted to Russian Orthodoxy in 1912. From the spring of 1913 to the summer of 1914, Frank took a sabbatical leave to Germany, where he wrote his first important philosophical work, *The Object of Knowledge,* published in 1915.[4] In *The Object of Knowledge,* Frank sets for himself the goal of elucidating the ontological conditions of the possibility of intuition as an immediate knowledge of being independent of our acts of knowing. This possibility is explained by the rootedness of individual being in the Absolute as Total Unity. Owing to this rootedness in the Absolute,

---

3. Besides Frank, the contributors were P. B. Struve, Nikolai Berdiav, Sergey Bulgakov, M. O. Gershenzon, A. S. Izgoev, and B. A. Kistiakovsky.

4. See the bibliography attached to this introduction for a listing of Frank's major philosophical works and translations of these works into English.

every object, prior to all knowledge of it, is close to us in complete immediacy, since we are fused with it not through our consciousness but in our very being.

Frank passed the years of the Great War in Petersburg. In 1916 he wrote, and in 1917 published, his major work on philosophical psychology, *Man's Soul*, intended to be a complement to *The Object of Knowledge*. The reform of "gnoseology" (the theory of knowledge) into "first philosophy" or general ontology which Frank outlined in *The Object of Knowledge* necessitated the development of a philosophical psychology as a doctrine of the nature of the individual "soul" and the relation of the "soul" to supra-individual objective being.

From the summer of 1917 to the fall of 1921, Frank served as the dean of the historico-philosophical department of Saratov University. He would have preferred to stay in Petrograd, but the supply difficulties caused by the war and the revolution made it impossible for him to feed his family (his wife and three children). In 1921, Frank and his family moved to Moscow; this was at the beginning of the "New Economic Plan," which was accompanied by a short-lived cultural liberalization. Non-communist and even anti-communist intellectuals were allowed to function as academicians and to take part in literary and cultural groups. Frank was elected as a member of the Moscow Philosophical Institute and was one of the founders of the Academy of Spiritual Culture. One goal of this academy was to organize a series of public lectures on philosophical, religious, and general cultural themes, to be attended by various strata of the public, including students, workers, and Red Army soldiers. However, this liberalization ended quickly. The Politburo realized what was going on, and arrested and then expelled from the Soviet Union a large number of important scholars and writers, including Frank.

Frank's exile started in September 1922. He lived in Germany until 1937; he then moved to France, where he lived until 1945; finally, he went to England, where he lived until his death in 1950.

The years of exile were extremely productive. Frank's great work of this period was *The Unknowable: A Philosophical Introduction to the Ontology of Religion* (1938). In this work, Frank affirms that objective knowledge does not exhaust the structure of the world; mystical experience reveals to us a deeper domain of the world, something not expressible in concepts, something "unknowable," about which one can have knowledge only in the form of "wise ignorance" (Nicholas of Cusa's *docta ignorantia*). Frank explores this domain in three strata of being: in objective being, in our own being, and in that stratum of reality which, as the primordial ground and total unity (identified with Divinity), unites and grounds both objective being and our own being.

The other major work published by Frank during this time was *The Spiritual Foundations of Society* (1930). This work is an attempt to explore and define the spiritual nature of society, to investigate society as a type of being, i.e., to develop an ontology of society. Frank finds the presence of two strata in society: the inner stratum consists in the unity of "we," while the outer one consists in the decomposition of this unity into the separateness, opposition, and antagonism of many "I's." This duality leads to the opposition between the inner organicity and the outer mechanicity of society, to the dualities of morality and law, grace and the law, and the church and the world.

In 1933, when the Nazis came to power, Frank, since he was of Jewish descent, lost the ability to earn a living in Germany. And when the Gestapo began to take an interest in him, he emigrated to France. When the Second World War started in 1939, Frank, his wife, and one son were cut off from the rest of the family — his other two children, who were living in England. The war years were very hard for Frank. Hunger and mortal danger from the Germans in Petain's government, anxiety about his children, and the consciousness that Europe had fallen under the power of unchained evil — these were the shadows under which Frank lived and worked during 1939 to 1945.

The two major works of this period were religious ones: *God with Us* and *The Light Shineth in Darkness*. In *God with Us,* Frank expounds the principles of Christianity and shows that the entire substantial content of Christianity is grounded on religious experience, on "the meeting between man's heart and God." God is love, and Christianity teaches man to carry out the sacrifice of love and, like the God-man Jesus Christ, to follow the way of the cross. In *The Light Shineth in Darkness,* the recognition that sin wields an enormous power in the world is combined with "faith in the positive value of the world as a creation of God and as an expression . . . of the holy essence of God."[5] This combination leads to a clear distinction between Christ's absolute truth and its always imperfect embodiment in the world — between the essential salvation of the world and its protection from evil. On the other hand, it leads to a perception of the nature of moral creative activity as a dramatic Divine-human process of the healing of the world through the imbedding in it of its Divine primordial ground and the battle against dark human willfulness. Insofar as man has come to believe in the glad tidings of the Kingdom and has surrendered himself to the action of the Divine gracious powers that pour down upon him together with these tidings, he is a participant in the gracious Divine-human being, and his participation in this being forms the foundation and true essence of his entire human existence. Man is a creature of light; and the darkness of the world cannot destroy him.

3

Frank wrote *The Meaning of Life* in the period immediately following his expulsion from the Soviet Union in 1922. It grew out of an extraordinary polemical work, *The Fall of the Idols* (1923);[6] indeed, the two works (both addressed to the Russian Christian youth in the emigration) can be considered as two volumes of a single work, exploring the plight of the world in the early 1920s.

The Fall of the Idols is a substantially expanded version of a speech that Frank gave in May 1923 at a conference of Russian students in Germany, organized by the American Young Men's Christian Association. Frank later recalled that, during these years, he had devoted himself entirely to the sphere of spiritual life and spiritual interests — to the work of the inner verification and deepening of the spiritual foundations of his own worldview and to the social work of spiritually influencing young people. For Frank, it became clear that Russia could be reborn only by this kind of spiritual activity, not by any political action. And a major ele-

5. S. L. Frank, *The Light Shineth in Darkness*, trans. Boris Jakim (Athens: Ohio University Press, 1989), p. xxiii.

6. The concluding chapter of *The Fall of the Idols* (Russian title: *Krushenie Kumirov*) is provided in the Appendix to the present volume.

ment of this spiritual work consisted in the destruction of the "idols" that formerly had contaminated the minds and ruined the lives of the Russian intelligentsia: the idol of the revolution, the idol of politics, the idol of culture, and the idol of moral idealism. In other words, the "idols" are what stand between us and the true meaning of life, between us and the living God. *The Fall of the Idols* is concerned with showing how these idols have already collapsed and that those who still worship them will themselves perish. *The Fall of the Idols* presents a negative critique of the situation of humanity in general (and of the situation of the Russian nation in particular) in the early 1920s.

The Meaning of Life, on the other hand, offers positive solutions and positive pathways that humanity might follow if it is to regain, or to find for the first time, "the meaning of life." *The Meaning of Life* is a transitional work, representing a change in the type of philosophy that Frank was doing. With this work, he stops writing what can be called "pure" philosophy and moves on to a religious philosophy formed in the crucible of his personal suffering and the suffering of the Russian people. He moves on from the theoretical philosophy of such works as *The Object of Knowledge* and *Man's Soul* to the major books of the émigré period: *The Spiritual Foundations of Society, The Unknowable,* and *The Light Shineth in Darkness.* In *The Meaning of Life* we find adumbrations of these three great works of religious philosophy; it is the seed from which they sprouted, as it were. The experience of the Russian Revolution and the collapse of Russia changed Frank: he could no longer concern himself only with questions of epistemology and philosophical speculation. He became preoccupied with how philosophy can help us find the meaning of life and thus help to save humanity in its hour of horror and need.

Yes, *The Meaning of Life* is a book about suffering. It is the closest thing we have in the twenty-first century to the book of Job. Frank and his fellow Russians lost everything — their homes, their families, their native land, their work, their sense of self — and now they must make sense of their lives and find out if anything at all has meaning.

Frank takes the sufferings of the Russian people and raises them to a metaphysics, a theodicy. Like Job, Frank will not be consoled with earthly consolations. He is seeking the living God, and this living God is the greatest boon, and worth infinitely more than all that has been lost.

In seeking the meaning of life, what does Frank find? He finds that the meaning of life is the indissoluble unity of perfect fulfillment and perfect clarity, the unity of light and Truth. It is the absolutely firm foundation of our life; it is the perfect illumination of life. This is how Frank put it:

> Life becomes meaningful to the extent that it freely and consciously serves the absolute and supreme good. This good is eternal *life*, quickening human life and serving as the eternal foundation and true fulfillment of the latter; and it is also absolute truth, the light of reason, permeating and illuminating human life. Our life attains meaning to the extent that it is a rational path to a goal, or a path to the rational supreme goal; otherwise, it is a meaningless and errant wandering. But such a true path for our life can only be that which at the same time is both life and Truth: "I am the way, the truth, and the life" (John 14:6).[7]

* * *

Bibliography to the Works of S. L. Frank

WORKS BY FRANK

Predmet znaniya: Ob osnovakh i predelakh otvlechyonnovo znaniya (The Object of Knowledge: On the Foundations and Limits of Abstract Knowledge). St. Petersburg, 1915.

Dusha cheloveka: Opyt vvedeniia v filosofskuyu psikhologiyu. Moscow, 1917. Translated by Boris Jakim as *Man's Soul: An Introductory Essay in Philosophical Psychology.* Athens: Ohio University Press, 1993.

Dukhovye osnovy obshchestva: Vvedenie v sotsial'nuyu filosofiyu. Paris, 1930. Translated by Boris Jakim as *The Spiritual Foundations of Society: An Introduction to Social Philosophy.* Athens: Ohio University Press, 1987.

Nepostizhimoye: Ontologicheskoye vvedenie v filosofiyu religii. Paris, 1939. Translated by Boris Jakim as *The Unknowable: An Ontological Introduction to the Philosophy of Religion.* Athens: Ohio University Press, 1983.

---

7. See p. 35 of the present volume.

Svet vo T'me: Opyt khristianskopi etiki is sotsial'noi filosofii. Paris, 1949. Translated by Boris Jakim as *The Light Shineth in Darkness: An Essay in Christian Ethics and Social Philosophy.* Athens: Ohio University Press, 1989.

Real'nost i chelovek. Paris, 1956. Translated by Natalie Duddington as *Reality and Man.* London: Faber & Faber, 1965.

S nami Bog: Tri razmyshleniya. Paris, 1964. Translated by Natalie Duddington as *God with Us: Three Meditations.* London: Jonathan Cape, 1946.

WORKS ON FRANK

Boobbyer, Philip. *S. L. Frank: The Life and Work of a Russian Philosopher, 1877-1950.* Athens: Ohio University Press, 1995. This is the best biography of Frank in any language.

Lossky, N. O. *History of Russian Philosophy.* New York, 1951. Pp. 266-92.

Zenkovsky, V. V. *Istoriia russkoi filosofii,* 2 vols. Paris, 1948, 1950. Translated by George L. Kline as *A History of Russian Philosophy,* 2 vols. London and New York, 1953. Vol. 2, pp. 852-72.

Zenkovsky, V. V., ed. *Sbornik pamyati Semena Lyudvigovicha Frank (A Collection of Essays in Memory of Simon Ludvigovich Frank).* Munich, 1954.

Author's Preface

The present book, long in the planning, is a natural continuation, as it were, of a little book I published in 1924: *The Fall of the Idols.*[1] *The Meaning of Life* was written in response to the oft-repeated advice of friends and colleagues that I should produce a work that would disclose the positive content of ideas that, in *The Fall of the Idols,* were expounded primarily in the form of a critique of prevailing prejudices. This second book, like the first, being an expression of the author's personal beliefs, grew in connection with conversations and arguments that arose in the circle of the Russian Student Christian Movement.[2] Therefore, *The Meaning of Life* is, in the first place, offered to the attention of the young participants of this Movement and in general to Russian youths in the emigration.

It is this that has determined the style of the book: The author has attempted to express his religio-philosophical ideas in a form that is as simple and accessible as possible, and to discuss only that which has essential significance for our lives.

Berlin,
29 August 1925

---

1. The concluding chapter of *The Fall of the Idols* (Russian title: *Krushenie kumirov*) is presented in the Appendix to the present volume. For a discussion of this work and its relationship to *The Meaning of Life,* see the Translator's Foreword. *Trans.*

2. This movement arose in the early 1920s among Russian émigrés in Europe with the aim of promoting Christian ideas and a Christian way of life among young Russians. *Trans.*

Introduction

D oes life have a meaning, and if it does, what exactly is this meaning? What is the meaning of life? Or is life just a meaningless and insignificant process of the natural birth, blossoming, maturation, decay, and death of man, as well as of every other limited being? From our early years our souls are troubled by dreams of goodness and of truth, of the spiritual significance and meaning of our lives, and these dreams compel us to think that we have been born not "for nothing," that we are called to realize something great and decisive in the world and thus to actualize ourselves as well, to give a creative outlet to those spiritual powers in us which form as if the true essence of our "I," but which now only slumber in us, are hidden from external sight, but insistently demand that they be revealed. Do these dreams have any kind of objective justification? Do they have any kind of rational foundation, and if they do, what is it? Or are they merely little flames of blind passion which flare up in a living being in accordance with the natural laws of this being's nature? Are they merely elemental strivings and yearnings by means of which indifferent nature, deceiving and seducing us with illusions, uses us to accomplish its meaningless, eternally repetitive, and monotonous task of the preservation of animal life in the succession of generations? The human thirst for love and happiness, tears of delight in the presence of beauty, the tremulous thought of luminous joy illuminating and warming life or rather realizing true life for the first time — is there any solid foundation for this in man's being, or is this only a reflection in man's feverish consciousness of that blind and obscure passion which controls even the insects, which, deceiving us, uses us as instruments to preserve that very same meaningless prose of animal life, and which as payment for our brief dream of higher joy and spiritual fullness condemns us to a narrow, boring, and banal existence tormented by need? And the thirst for holy exploit, for self-renouncing service of the good, the thirst for self-sacrifice in the name of a great and luminous task — does this represent anything greater and more meaningful than the mysterious but meaningless force which chases the moth into the flame?

These "accursed" questions, as they are usually called, or rather this one question "concerning the meaning of life," trouble and torment every human being in the depths of his soul. For a period of time, and even for a very long period, one can completely forget about this question. It is possible to submerge oneself in the ordinary and pressing interests of the present day, in material cares directed at the preservation of life, at the attainment of riches, contentment, or earthly success. It is also possible to submerge oneself in suprapersonal passions and "works" — in politics, the battle of parties, and so on. But life is arranged in such a way that not even the most obtuse, materially "fat," and spiritually asleep man can avoid this question totally and forever: The inexorable fact of the approach of death and of its inevitable precursors, of aging and sicknesses, the fact of dying, of disappearance, of submergence into the irretrievable past of our entire earthly life with all the illusory significance of its interests — this fact is for every human being a dread and persistent reminder of the unanswered question that he has been avoiding: the question concerning the *meaning of life*. This question is not a "theoretical question"; it is not the object of an idle game of the mind. It is a question of life itself. It is just as frightening and, strictly speaking, even much more frightening than the question of obtaining a piece of bread to sate one's hunger when one is in dire need. Truly, it is a question concerning bread that could sate us and concerning water that could quench our thirst. In one of his stories, Chekhov describes a man who has spent his entire life in a provincial town and occupied himself with petty cares, a man who, like all other men, lied and pretended, "played a role" in "society," concerned himself with "business," was immersed in petty intrigues and cares. But suddenly and unexpectedly, he awoke one night with a rapid heartbeat and in a cold sweat. What had happened? Something terrible had happened: *life had passed.* And there was no life because it had and has no meaning!

Nevertheless, the overwhelming majority of people consider it necessary to avoid this question, to hide from it. They find that the supreme life-wisdom consists in such a "politics of the ostrich," which buries its head in the ground. They call this a "fundamental rejection" of the attempt to answer "unanswerable metaphysical questions," and they so skillfully deceive all others and themselves that, not only for the outside observer but also for them themselves, their torment and insatiable longing sometimes remain unnoticed until the very hour of death. This tactic of educating oneself and others to forget the most important — and in the final analysis the only important — question of life is, however, determined not solely by the "politics of the ostrich," by the desire to shut one's eyes to the terrible truth. Apparently, the ability "to arrange one's life," to obtain the goods of life, to assert and expand one's position in the struggle of life — this ability is inversely proportional to the attention given to the question of "the meaning of life." And since, in virtue of man's animal nature and the "common sense" determined by this animal nature, this ability appears to be the most important and urgent thing in life, it is in the interests of this ability that the troubling perplexity about the meaning of life is repressed deep into the recesses of the unconscious. And the depth of the inner psychical grave into which the question of the meaning of life is buried is directly proportional to the tranquility and order of our external life, to our preoccupation with current earthly interests and the success with which we realize these interests. Thus, for example, we see that the "average European," the typical Western-European "bourgeois" (not in the economic but in the spiritual sense of the word), appears to have lost all interest in this question and thus has stopped needing religion, which alone can provide an answer to it. We Russians — in part because of our nature and in part evidently because of the chaotic character of our external, civil, quotidian, and social life — differed from Western Europeans even in the earlier, "happier" times by the fact that we were more acutely tormented by the question of the meaning of life, or were more openly tormented by it, were more frank in admitting that we were tormented by it. However, now, looking back at our past, which is so recent and at the same time so remote from us,[1] we must confess that even then we had grown "fat" with material things and did not see — did not wish to see and could not see — the true face of life, and therefore concerned ourselves little with solving the enigma of life.

This horrifying destruction of our entire social life has brought us, precisely from this point of view, one precious good: it has revealed to us *life as it really is.* True, from the common, everyday point of view, from the point of view of ordinary, earthly "life wisdom," we are often tormented by the *abnormality* of our present life and tend to do one of two things: either, with infinite hatred, we blame this abnormality on the Bolsheviks, who senselessly cast all Russian people into an abyss of calamity and despair; or (and this is of course better) with bitter and useless repentance we condemn our own thoughtlessness, negligence, and blindness, through which we permitted the destruction of all the foundations of a normal, happy, and rational life in Russia. These bitter feelings may contain a certain degree of relative truth, but — in the face of the ultimate, genuine truth — they also contain a very dangerous self-deception. In surveying the loss of our dear ones, either murdered outright or killed by the savage conditions of life, or the loss of our property, of our beloved work; in surveying our premature sicknesses, the forced inactivity and meaninglessness of our present existence, we often think that sicknesses, death, old age, need, and the meaninglessness of life were invented by the Bolsheviks. However, in fact they did not invent all these things, but only significantly intensified them, having destroyed that external and — from a more profound point of view — nevertheless illusory well-being which had previously reigned in life. Even prior to the Bolsheviks, people had died, and they had almost always died prematurely, meaninglessly, and accidentally, and without completing their work. Even prior to the Bolsheviks, all the goods of life — riches, health, glory, social standing — had been unstable and unreliable. Even prior to the Bolsheviks, the wisdom of the Russian people knew that no one could be certain of avoiding prison or the beggar's pouch.

That which has occurred has only ripped the veil of illusion from life

1. Frank is writing this in the early 1920s and is referring to the gulf caused by the Revolution between the world of Tsarist Russia and that of the Russians in exile. *Trans.*

4

and shown us its true horror: it has shown us how life always is in itself. Just as the motion pictures employ a distortion caused by an arbitrary change in the rate of motion to show the true nature of motion, which is imperceptible to our ordinary vision; and just as a magnifying glass enables us to see for the first time that which always exists and has always existed but which is invisible to the unaided eye, so the distortion of the "normal" empirical conditions of life which has now occurred in Russia reveals to us the hitherto-concealed true essence of life. And we Russians, who, without work and purpose, without homeland and hearth, are now languishing in poverty in foreign lands or living in our homeland as if in a foreign land; we Russians, conscious of all the "abnormality" of our present existence from the point of view of the usual external forms of life — we nevertheless have the right and obligation to say that it is precisely this abnormal form of life which for the first time has enabled us to know the true eternal essence of life. We are homeless wanderers and without refuge, but is not man always, in the profoundest sense, a homeless wanderer on earth and without refuge? We have experienced upon ourselves and upon our loved ones, upon our most intimate being and upon our career, the greatest vicissitudes of fate, but is it not the very essence of fate to be full of vicissitudes? We have felt the closeness and the dread reality of death, but is this a reality only of the present day? In the midst of the luxurious and carefree life of the Russian royal court of the eighteenth century, the Russian poet exclaims, "Where once a feast was spread, now a coffin lies./The place where festive singing rang/ Now hears but graveside keening,/And pale death watches over all."[2] We are condemned to heavy, exhausting labor for our daily bread, but was not Adam already told and commanded, at his expulsion from Eden, "In the sweat of thy face shall thou eat bread" (Gen. 3:19)?

And so, through the magnifying glass of our present woes, there has clearly been revealed to us the very essence of life with all its vicissitudes and in all its briefness and arduousness — in all its meaninglessness. And for this reason the question of the meaning of life — the unavoidable question which torments all men — has acquired a completely excep-

---

2. These lines are from Gavril Derzhavin's poem titled "On the Death of Prince Meshchersky." *Trans.*

tional acuteness for us, for us who have, as it were, come to know for the first time the very essence of life and are deprived of the possibility of hiding from it or veiling it with an illusory appearance that softens its horror. It was easy not to think about this question when life, at least the external and visible life, flowed evenly and smoothly, when — if we exclude the relatively rare moments of tragic trials, which appeared to us exceptional and abnormal — life seemed tranquil and stable, when each of us had his natural and rational work, and when — behind a multitude of questions of the present day, behind a multitude of particular matters and questions vital and important for us — the general question of life as a whole only glimmered somewhere in the far-off distances and obscurely and secretly troubled us. Particularly in our youth, at a time when one thinks that all the questions of life will be resolved in the future, at a time when one is filled with an overabundance of vital forces which require, and often find, application, at a time when the conditions of life easily permit one to live by dreams, only a few of us acutely suffered from the consciousness of the meaninglessness of life.

That is not the case now. Having lost our homeland and, with it, the natural soil for work which gives at least the appearance of meaning to life; and deprived of the possibility of the carefree youthful enjoyment of life and of the possibility of forgetting about its pitiless severity in this elemental surrender to its temptations, we are condemned to a heavy, slave labor for our daily bread — we are compelled to ask ourselves: What are we living for? Why are we pulling this absurd and painful load? What justifies our suffering? Where will we find an unshakable support which will keep us from falling beneath the weight of need?

It is true that the majority of Russians are still trying to chase away such dreadful and painful thoughts by the passionate dream of the future renewal and regeneration of our common Russian life. Russians have always had the habit of living by dreams about the future: even earlier it had seemed to them that the workaday, severe, and dim life of the present day was actually a chance misunderstanding, a temporary interruption in the arrival of true life, an agonizing wait, something like the annoying wait on a train that has stopped moving for some chance reason. But tomorrow, or in a few years, or sometime soon in the future, everything will change — a true, rational, and happy life will be revealed. The whole meaning of life is in this future, and the present day is of no importance for life. Such dreams and their effect on the moral will, this lack of moral seriousness, this contempt for and indifference to the present, this inwardly untrue and groundless idealization of the future — this spiritual condition is precisely the ultimate root of that moral sickness which is called the *revolutionary* attitude, and this sickness is what ruined Russian life. But this spiritual condition has perhaps never been as widespread as it is today; and one must admit that there has never been as much justification for such a condition as there is at the present time. After all, it is impossible to deny that sooner or later the day will finally come when Russian life will rise out of the quagmire into which it has sunk and in which it now finds itself in a state of frozen inertia. It is impossible to deny that this will be a day that not only will ease the personal conditions of our lives but — and this is much more important — that will also place us into healthier and more normal social conditions, that will reveal the possibility of rational work, that will revitalize our powers by plunging our roots once again into our native soil.

Nevertheless, even at the present time this attitude of transferring the question of the meaning of life from the present day to the longed-for and unknown future, of expecting this question to be resolved not through the inner spiritual energy of our own will but by unforeseeable changes produced by fate; this utter contempt for and capitulation before the present associated with the dreamy idealization of the future — this attitude remains the same psychical and moral sickness that it always has been, the same distortion of the healthy relation — rooted in man's spiritual essence — to reality and to the tasks of one's life. And the exceptional intensity of this attitude attests only to the acuteness of our sickness. The circumstances of our life are falling together in such a way that this is becoming increasingly clear to us.

The arrival of this decisive radiant day, which for a long time we had been expecting to arrive practically in a day or two, is now delayed into the distant future; and the longer we wait for it and as more of our hopes turn out to be illusory, the more uncertain seems the possibility of its arrival: this day recedes for us beyond the visible horizon; we now expect it to come not tomorrow or the day after tomorrow, but only "in a few years," and no one is able to foretell how many years we must wait for it, nor why or under what conditions it will arrive. And many people are beginning to think that this longed-for day will, perhaps, not come in a perceptible fashion, that it will not be a sharp and absolute boundary between the hated present and the radiant, joyous future, but that Russian life will begin to return to a more normal state only imperceptibly and gradually, perhaps through a series of small changes. And given the total impenetrability of the future for us, given the erroneousness of all our previous predictions, which had repeatedly promised the arrival of the blessed day, it is impossible to deny the likelihood or at least the possibility of such an outcome. But as soon as we admit this possibility, we must reject the spiritual position according to which genuine life will not be realized until the arrival of this decisive day.

But even apart from this consideration, should we and can we *wait* for a long period of time, and is it possible for us to spend our entire life in an inactive and meaningless period of *waiting* of unspecified length? The older generation of Russians is beginning to come to terms with the bitter thought that it will perhaps not live to see this day or at best will see its arrival only in old age, when the entirety of one's active life will be in the past. The younger generation is beginning to realize, at the very least, that the best years of its life are passing and perhaps will pass totally in such a period of waiting. And if only we still had the possibility of spending our lives not in the meaningless and painful wait for this day but in the active preparation for this day; if only we still had the possibility — as in the previous epoch — of revolutionary action, and not only revolutionary dreams and outpourings of words! But this possibility is absent for the vast majority of Russians, and we see clearly that many of those who think they possess this possibility are in error precisely because, poisoned by this sickness of dreaminess, they have forgotten how to distinguish genuine, serious, productive *work* from mere outpourings of words, from meaningless and infantile tempests in a glass of water.

Thus, fate itself — or the immense superhuman forces that we dimly perceive behind blind fate — is curing us of this comforting but corrupting sickness which consists in the dreamy transposition of the question of life and of its meaning into the indeterminate distances of the future. It is curing us of the cowardly and illusory hope that someone or something in the external world will resolve this question for us. At the present time the majority of us have, if not a clear awareness, then at least a dim feeling that the question of the awaited regeneration of our homeland and of the associated improvement of the lot of each of us is by no means in competition with the question of how and for what purpose we are to live today — in that *today* which is stretching over long years and which can extend over our entire life. Nor is it in competition with the question of the eternal and absolute meaning of life as such: it does not by any means eclipse this most important and essential question. Furthermore, this awaited future "day" will, after all, not automatically produce a new organization of all of Russian life and automatically create more rational conditions for the latter. This re-organization of Russian life will have to be accomplished by Russians themselves, *including each of us.* But what happens if, during this painful period of waiting, we expend the entire reserve of our spiritual energies? What happens if, uselessly wasting our lives on meaningless and aimless yearnings during this period, we lose a clear idea of good and evil, of what forms of life are desirable and what forms are unworthy? Can we renew our communal life if we as individuals do not know what we are living for and what the eternal, objective meaning of life in its entirety is? Do we not already see that many Russians, having despaired at finding a resolution to the question of the meaning of life, are succumbing to spiritual stupor and inertia and devoting themselves to the banal task of earning their daily bread? Do we not see that others are choosing suicide, while still others are dying morally, out of despair burning their lives at both ends, committing crimes and surrendering to moral corruption in order to find self-forgetfulness in savage pleasures, even though their cold souls are well aware of the vulgarity and transience of these pleasures?

No, the question of the meaning of life is something we — precisely we, in our present situation and spiritual condition — cannot escape; and vain are all our attempts to replace this question with various kinds of surrogates, to appease the worm of doubt gnawing inside us with various illusory deeds and thoughts. Precisely our era is such (we have already discussed this in our book *The Fall of the Idols*[3]) that all the idols

---

3. See the Translator's Foreword and the Author's Preface for a discussion of this book. Its concluding chapter is presented in the Appendix to the present volume. *Trans.*

that had previously tempted and blinded us are collapsing one after the other, exposed in their falsehood: All the veils that had prettified and obscured life are falling; all the illusions are fading. What remains is life itself, life in all its unsightly nakedness, with all its painfulness and meaninglessness — life which is equivalent to death and non-being, but which does not have the peace and forgetting associated with non-being. On the heights of Sinai, God imposed, through ancient Israel, a task upon all people and for all times: "I have set before you life and death, blessing and cursing: therefore choose life, that both thou and thy seed may live" (Deut. 30:19). This task of learning to distinguish true life from life which is death, of understanding that meaning of life which for the first time makes life life, that Word of God which is the true bread of life that sates us — this task confronts us so inexorably precisely in this period of great catastrophes, of God's great punishment upon us, owing to which all the curtains are torn and all of us have once again "fallen into the hands of the living God." This task confronts us with such pitiless and terrible clarity that no one who has ever learned of it can evade the duty of fulfilling it.

"What Is to Be Done?"[1]

A s attested by the once-celebrated novel by Chernyshevsky,[2] Russian intellectuals have long been accustomed to posing the question of the "meaning of life" in the form of the question "What is to be done?"

The question "What is to be done?" can of course be posed in several very different senses. Its most definite and rational sense — one might say the only fully rational sense, admitting a precise answer — is that which implies the search for a *path* or *means* to some specific goal agreed upon in advance and indisputable for the questioner. One can ask what should be done in order to improve one's health, to earn an income that provides for one's subsistence, or to have success in society, and so on. And the most fruitful formulation of this question is that which possesses maximal concreteness; it can then often have a unique and fully grounded answer. Thus, to be sure, rather than posing the general question "What is to be done in order to be more healthy?" it is more fruitful to pose the question in the way we pose it when we are consulting a physician: "At my age and given my past history, my manner of life, and the general condition of my organism, what should I do to be cured of this or

1. This is a famous question in Russian history. Chernyshevsky, Tolstoy, and Lenin all wrote books with this title. *Trans.*

2. Nikolai Chernyshevsky (1828-1889), Russian literary and social critic, was the guiding spirit of Russian nihilism and a major representative of positivistic materialism in nineteenth-century Russian philosophy. In 1863 he published the tendentious radical novel *What Is to Be Done? Trans.*

that specific ailment?" And all analogous questions should be formulated in this manner. It would be easier to find an answer, and the answer would be more precise, if questions about the means of attaining health, material well-being, success in love, and so on were posed in a fully concrete form which takes into account all the particular, individual properties of the questioner himself, as well as his environment, and if (and this is the main thing) the very goal of his striving were not something indeterminately general, like health or riches *in general,* but something fully concrete, like the healing of a specific sickness, income from a specific profession, and so on. "What should I do in a given case in order to attain a given concrete goal?" is a kind of question we pose every day; and every step of our practical lives is a result of our resolution of one of these questions. It does not make any sense to discuss the meaning and legitimacy of the question "What is to be done?" in such a completely concrete and rationally practical form.

And of course *this* meaning of the question does not have anything in common, except the verbal expression, with that agonizing sense — requiring a fundamental resolution and usually not finding it — in which this question is posed when for the questioner himself it is identical with the question of the meaning of his life. It is then, first of all, a question not about the means to attaining a specific goal but about the very goal of life and activity. But in this formulation too the question can be posed in various senses which substantially differ from one another. Thus, in one's youth, one inevitably deals with the question of choosing a single life-path from among many possibilities that present themselves. "What am I to do?" in this case means "What special life-work, what profession should I choose, or how do I determine what my vocation is?" "What am I to do?" implies questions of the following kind: Should I, for example, enroll in a university, or should I enter the work world right away, learn a craft, work at a trade, or work in an office? And if I choose to enroll in a university, what should I specialize in? Should I prepare myself for the profession of a physician, an engineer, an agronomist? Of course, here too one can find the right answers to such questions only by taking into account all the concrete conditions, those pertaining to the person asking the questions (his inclinations and abilities, his health, the strength of his will, etc.) as well as the external conditions of his life (his material resources, the relative difficulty — in the given country and at the given time — of the various life paths considered, the relative profitability of one profession or another, again at the given time and in the given place, etc.).

But the main thing is that a definite and true answer to the question is possible only if the questioner already clearly knows the final goal of his strivings, only if he has a clear idea of what the highest and most important value of life is for him. He must first of all evaluate himself and decide what is most important for him in this choice: he must decide what motives are guiding him, whether in choosing a profession or life path he is primarily seeking material security, prominence, and a high social position, or the fulfillment of the inner (and in this case, which precisely?) requirements of his personality. And so here too it becomes clear that we only appear to be resolving the question of the goal of our life, whereas in reality we are only discussing different means or paths to some goal which is already known to us. Consequently, questions of this kind, in the capacity of purely practical and rational questions concerning the means to a particular goal, can also be classified as questions of the aforementioned type, although here one has in view not the purposiveness of a particular, individual step or action but the purposiveness of a general definition of constant conditions and of a constant sphere of life and activity.

In the precise sense, the question "What am I to do?" (meaning "Toward what should I strive?" or "What life goal should I set for myself?") is posed when the questioner is not clearly aware of the content of the higher, ultimate, all-determining goal and value of life. But here too there can exist very significant differences in the meaning of the question. In the case of each *individual* statement of the question — "What am *I, personally,* to do?" or "What goal or value should *I,* personally, choose for *myself* as the goal that determines my life?" — it is tacitly assumed that there exists a certain complex hierarchy of goals and values and a corresponding innate hierarchy of persons; and it is assumed that every person (and first of all — I) seeks his appropriate place in this system, seeks in this polyphonic chorus the proper voice that corresponds to *his own* personality. In this case the question is reducible to the question of self-knowledge, to a clarification of *my* proper vocation, of the role in the universe that has been assigned precisely to *me* by nature or Providence. Without any doubt, the hierarchy of goals or values and a general conception of this hierarchy's content *as a whole* remain present here.

Only now have we arrived, by rejecting all of its other meanings, at the meaning of the question "What is to be done?" in which it directly implies the question of the meaning of life. When I pose the question not about what I am *personally* to do (even if this is in the higher sense that we have just pointed out — in the sense of which goal or value I must recognize as determining for my life) but about what is to be done *in general* or by all people, then I have in mind a doubt that is directly connected with the question of the meaning of life. Life in its immediate flow, determined by elemental forces, is meaningless. What must be done, how should life be organized in order to make it *meaningful?* — that is what the doubt here consists of. What is the unique *work* or *activity,* common to all people, which illuminates life with meaning and through participation in which my life too, consequently, acquires meaning for the first time?

That is the typically Russian meaning of the question "What is to be done?" In its Russian sense, we can express this question more precisely as follows: "What can I and others do *to save the world, thus justifying our life for the first time?*" This question is based on a series of premises which can be expressed roughly as follows: The world in its immediate, empirical being and flow is meaningless; it is perishing from sufferings, deprivations, moral evil — from egotism, hatred, and injustice. All simple participation in the life of the world, in the sense of the simple involvement in the elemental forces whose collision determines its flow, is a co-participation in meaningless chaos by virtue of which the participant's own life is only a meaningless aggregation of blind and burdensome external accidents. But human beings are collectively called to *transfigure* the world and to *save* it, to organize it in such a way that its supreme goal could be truly realized in it. And the question consists in how to find that *work* or *activity,* common to all people, which would accomplish the salvation of the world. In other words, in this case "What is to be done?" means "How can the world be re-made in such a way that one could realize absolute truth and absolute meaning in it?"

Russians suffer from the meaninglessness of life. They acutely feel that if all they do is "live like everybody else," if all they do is eat, drink, marry, work to feed their family, and even enjoy ordinary human happiness, they then live in a dark, meaningless vortex, carried like a piece of wood by the current of time; and in the face of the inevitable end of life, they do not know why they have lived on earth. They feel with their whole being that it is not enough to "simply live" — one must live *for something.* And the typical Russian intellectual thinks that "to live for something" is to live in order to participate in some great common work which perfects the world and leads it to final salvation. But the Russian intellectual does not know what should constitute this unique work, common to all people; and it is in this sense that he asks, "What is to be done?"

For the overwhelming majority of the Russian intelligentsia of the previous epoch, extending from the 1860s and in part even from the 1840s up to the catastrophe of 1917, the question "What is to be done?" receives in this sense a unique and fully definite answer: It is necessary to improve the political and social conditions of the life of the people, to remove that sociopolitical order whose defectiveness is causing the world to perish, and to introduce a new order which will assure the kingdom of justice and happiness on earth and thus bring true meaning into life. And a large number of Russians of this type firmly believed that the revolutionary destruction of the old order and the introduction of a new, democratic and socialistic order would lead to the immediate and everlasting attainment of this goal of life. They attempted to attain this goal with extraordinary stubbornness, passion, and self-sacrifice; without thinking of the consequences, they crippled their own lives and those of others — and *they did attain their goal!*

And when the goal was attained, when the old order was overthrown, when socialism was firmly established, it turned out that not only was the world not saved, not only did the world not become meaningful, but that in place of the previous life, which might have been meaningless from the absolute point of view but which was relatively well-adjusted and ordered, and which at least allowed the possibility of *seeking* what was better — in place of the previous life there arose total and complete meaninglessness, a chaos of blood, hatred, evil, and absurdity. Life had become hell. At the present time many believe — in perfect analogy with the past and only changing the content of the political ideal — that the salvation of the world consists in "the overthrow of the Bolsheviks," in the re-establishment of the old social forms, which now, after they have been lost, appear to be profoundly meaningful and able to return to life the meaning it has lost. The struggle for the restoration of past forms of life, whether it be the recent past of the political power of the Russian Empire or the remote past of the ideal of "Holy Russia" as it was supposedly realized in the epoch of the Muscovite Empire, or more generally and broadly, the realization of rational sociopolitical forms of life hallowed by ancient traditions — this struggle becomes the sole work that gives meaning to life, the general answer to the question, "What is to be done?"

Alongside this Russian spiritual type there is another, essentially kindred type. For this kindred type, the question "What is to be done?" receives the answer "It is necessary to perfect oneself morally." The world can and must be saved; its meaninglessness can be replaced by meaning, if every person will attempt to live not by blind passions but "rationally," in harmony with the moral ideal. A typical example of such a tendency is "Tolstoyanism,"[3] which is partially and unconsciously professed by many Russians who are not avowed "Tolstoyans." The "work" which in this case must save the world is not external political and social activity (and especially not violent revolutionary action) but the inner work of education performed upon oneself and others. However, the immediate goal of this activity is the same: to introduce into the world a new social order, new relations between people and forms of life, which will "save" the world; and often this order and these relations are conceived with a purely externally empirical content: vegetarianism, agricultural labor, and so on. But even given the most profound and subtle understanding of this "work" — namely, as the inner work of moral improvement — the general premises of this tendency are the same: the work remains precisely a "work," that is, it remains a humanly conceived and humanly implemented plan-based reform of the world, liberating the world from evil and thereby giving meaning to life.

One could mention other variants, possible and actual, of this ten-

---

3. This is the moral doctrine based on the teaching of Leo Tolstoy. *Trans.*

dency, but this is not significant for our goal. What is important for us here is not to examine and resolve the question "What is to be done?" in the sense indicated here, not to evaluate different possible *answers* to this question, but to clarify the meaning and value of the very posing of the question. In this posing the different variants of answers converge. At the basis of all these answers there lies the direct conviction that there is a unique great common work or activity which will save the world, and participation in which will for the first time give meaning to the life of the person. To what extent can one recognize such a posing of the question to be the correct path to the attainment of the meaning of life?

At the basis of this posing of the question, despite the fact that it has been distorted and is spiritually insufficient (which we presently intend to clarify), there undoubtedly lies a profound and genuine, although obscure, religious feeling. In its unconscious roots this posing of the question is united with the Christian hope of "a new heaven and a new earth." This posing of the question displays a correct understanding of the fact of the meaninglessness of life in its present condition and legitimately cannot become reconciled to this fact. In spite of this de facto meaninglessness, this posing of the question — believing in the possibility of attaining or realizing the meaning of life — thereby attests to its own (albeit unconscious) faith in principles and forces that are higher than this meaningless empirical life. But without giving itself an account of its necessary premises, in its conscious beliefs this posing of the question contains a number of contradictions and leads to a substantial distortion of the healthy, truly grounded relation to life.

First of all, this faith in the meaning of life acquired through participation in a great common work that is to save the world — this faith is unfounded. In truth, what is the basis here of this conviction that it is *possible* to save the world? If life, as it immediately is, is utterly meaningless, then from what source could there appear in it forces for inner self-correction, for the annihilation of this meaninglessness? It is evident that, in the combination of forces participating in the realization of the salvation of the world, this tendency presupposes some new principle, which is external to the empirical nature of life and which intrudes into life and corrects it. But where can this principle come from, and what is its proper essence?

Here this principle is — consciously or unconsciously — *man*; it is his striving for perfection, for the ideal; it is the moral forces of the good living in him. In this tendency we have an explicit or an implicit *humanism*. But what is man, and what is his significance in the world? What guarantees the possibility of human progress, of the gradual — or perhaps even sudden — achievement by man of perfection? What guarantees that human ideas of good and perfection are *true,* and that the moral efforts determined by these ideas will triumph over all the forces of evil, chaos, and blind passions? Let us not forget that, over the course of its entire history, mankind has aspired to this perfection, has passionately devoted itself to the dream of this perfection, and that to a certain degree its entire history is nothing else but the search for this perfection. All the same, we see now that this search was only a blind wandering, that it has not succeeded, and that immediate elemental life in all its meaninglessness has turned out to be undefeated.

What certainty can we have that precisely *we* will turn out to be happier or smarter than all our ancestors, that we will correctly define the work which will save life, and that we will be successful in realizing this work? After all, it is precisely our epoch, which — after the crushing, tragic failure of the passionate efforts of several Russian generations to save Russia and, through Russia, the entire world by means of democratic revolution and socialism — has received such an instructive lesson in this respect that it would appear that, from now on, it would be more natural for us to become more careful and skeptical in devising and realizing plans for the salvation of the world. And the reasons for this tragic collapse of our past dreams are now perfectly clear to us, if only we have the desire to attentively reflect upon them: They consisted not only in the erroneousness of the *plan* of salvation that was proposed but also in the inadequacy of the human material of the "saviors" (whether the "saviors" in question were the leaders of the movement or the people's masses which had faith in these leaders and which undertook to realize the imagined truth and to destroy evil).

We now see that these "saviors" immeasurably exaggerated, in their blind hatred, the evil of the past, the evil of the entire empirical, already realized life which surrounded them, and that they just as immeasurably exaggerated, in their blind pride, their own intellectual and moral powers. Moreover, the very erroneousness of the plan of salvation proposed by them was derived, in the final analysis, from this *moral* blindness of theirs. These proud "saviors" of the world, who opposed themselves and their aspirations, as the supreme rational and good principle, to the evil and chaos of all real life, these "saviors" themselves turned out to be a manifestation and product — and one of the worst products — of this evil and chaotic Russian reality. All the evil that had accumulated in Russian life — hatred and inattention to people, the bitterness of insult and injury, thoughtlessness and moral depravity, ignorance and gullibility, the spirit of repulsive and stupid willfulness, disrespect for law and justice — was expressed precisely in the "saviors" themselves, who considered themselves emissaries, as it were, come from another world to save Russia from evil and suffering.

What guarantees do we have at the present time that we, in our turn, will not end up in the pitiful and tragic role of "saviors" hopelessly enslaved and poisoned by the same evil and the same meaninglessness from which we desire to save others? But even irrespective of this terrible lesson, which, it would appear, must teach us to effect a substantial reform not only in the *content* of our moral-social ideal, but also in the very *structure* of our moral relation to life — even irrespective of this, the simple demand of logical consistency compels us to seek an answer to the following question: What is the basis of our faith in the rationality and victory of the forces which we think will overcome the meaninglessness of life if these forces themselves belong to the makeup of this very life? In other words, is it reasonable to believe that life itself, which is full of evil, will — by some inner process of self-purification and self-overcoming, by means of forces growing out of life itself — save itself, that the meaninglessness of the world will, in the person of man, overcome itself and implant in itself the kingdom of truth and meaning?

But let us for the time being set aside this alarming question, which clearly requires a negative answer. Let us even suppose that the dream of universal salvation, the dream of the establishment of the kingdom of good, reason, and justice in the world, can be realized by human powers, and that even at the present time we can participate in preparing its realization. The question would then arise: Will the future advent of this ideal and our participation in its realization liberate us from the meaninglessness of life? Will it give meaning to our life? Let us suppose that at some point in the future — whether remote or near — all people will be happy, good, and rational. But then what about the numberless generations that have descended into the grave? And what about us ourselves, who live now before the advent of this future state? What did they live for, and what are we living for now? Is it in order to prepare this future bliss? Let that be the case. But the past generations and we ourselves will not participate in this bliss; their life has passed and our life is passing without direct participation in it.

And so, what justifies our life? What gives it meaning? Is it really possible to consider meaningful the role of manure, serving to fertilize and prepare the future harvest? A man who uses manure for this purpose, *for himself,* acts of course in a meaningful way, but a man in *the role of manure* can scarcely be satisfied and can scarcely feel that his existence is meaningful. For if we believe that our life has a meaning or if we wish to find this meaning, then this in any case signifies (and we will return to this later in greater detail) that we propose to find in our life some absolute goal or value inherent in *it itself,* and not just a means for something else. The life of a slave is of course meaningful for the slave owner, who uses him like cattle, as an instrument for his enrichment; but it is absolutely meaningless for the slave himself as a subject of living self-consciousness, for the goal of this life has nothing to do with him as such a subject. And if nature or world history uses us as slaves for the purpose of enriching certain chosen ones — the future human generations — then our own life too is deprived of meaning.

The nihilist Bazarov in Turgenev's novel *Fathers and Children* speaks with perfect logical consistency when he says, "What business of mine is it whether or not peasants are happy if one day grass will grow out of me?" But it is not just *our* life which is meaningless in this case (although for us this is of course the main thing). Life in its entirety, *and therefore even the life of the future participants in the bliss of the "saved" world,* is also meaningless by virtue of this, and the world will by no means be saved by this triumph of the ideal condition sometime in the future. There is some sort of monstrous injustice, with which conscience and reason cannot reconcile themselves, in such an unequable distribution of good and evil, or reason and meaninglessness, between the living par-

20

ticipants in different world epochs — an injustice which makes life as a whole meaningless. Why must some suffer and die in darkness, while others, their future successors, are destined to enjoy the light of good and happiness? *For what purpose* is the world organized in such a *meaningless* way that the realization of justice in it must be preceded by a long period of injustice, and that a numberless multitude of people are condemned to spend their entire lives in this purgatory, in this agonizingly long "preparatory class" of mankind? Until we find an answer to this question, "For what purpose?" — until then the world will remain meaningless, and therefore its future bliss too will be meaningless. Indeed, it will be bliss only for those of its participants who are blind like animals and are capable of enjoying the present while forgetting about their connection with the past; whereas for thinking beings it cannot be bliss precisely because it will be poisoned by an endless anguish over past evil and past sufferings, by an unresolved doubt as to their meaning.

And so we face a pitiless dilemma. *Either* life as a whole *has meaning*, and then it must have meaning in each of its moments, for every generation of people and for every living human being, now, at this precise instant — absolutely without regard to all its possible changes and its supposed perfection in the future, inasmuch as this future is *only* the future and all of past life and present life do not participate in it. *Or* this is not the case, and life, our present life, *is meaningless* — and then there is no salvation from meaninglessness, and the entire future bliss of the world will not redeem and does not have the power to redeem this meaninglessness; and therefore there is also no salvation from this meaninglessness in our own striving toward this future, in our mental foretaste of this future and our active participation in its realization.

In other words, in thinking about life and its yearned-for meaning, we must inevitably be conscious of life as a *unified whole*. All of the world's life as a whole and our own brief life — not as a random fragment but as something which, despite its briefness and fragmentariness, is fused into a unity with the entirety of the world's life — this bi-unity of my "I" and the world must be recognized as an extratemporal and all-embracing whole; and about this whole we ask: Does it have a "meaning," and if it does, what does this meaning consist in? Therefore, the meaning of the world, the meaning of life, can never be realized in time; nor in general can it be associated with any time. Either this meaning *exists,* once and for all; or it *does not exist,* and this too holds once and for all.

At this point we are brought back to our earlier doubt about the possibility of the human realization of the salvation of the world; and we can fuse this doubt with our second doubt into one general negative result: *The world cannot remake itself.* It cannot, so to speak, get out of its own skin, or — unlike Baron Munchausen — it cannot pull itself out of the quagmire by its own hair, since this quagmire belongs to the world itself: the world is sinking in the quagmire only because the latter is contained in the world itself. And it is for this reason that man, as a part and a participant in the world's life, cannot accomplish any kind of "work" which would save him and give meaning to his life. The "meaning of life," whether it really exists or not, must be conceived in any case as some *eternal* principle; all things that occur in time, all things that appear and disappear, are parts and fragments of life as a whole and therefore cannot serve as the foundation of its meaning. Every work done by man is something derivative of him, of his life, of his spiritual nature, but the *meaning* of human life must in any case be something upon which man is grounded, something which serves as the one unchanging, absolutely stable *foundation* of his being.

All the works of a man and of mankind in general — both those which he himself considers great and that which he thinks is his unique and greatest work — are negligible and vain if he himself is negligible, if his life in essence has no meaning, if he is not rooted in some rational soil that surpasses him and is not created by him. Thus, although the meaning of life — if it exists! — gives meaning to human works and can inspire man to truly great works, no work by itself can give meaning to human life. To seek the missing meaning of life in some *work,* in the accomplishment of something, is to succumb to the illusion that man himself can create the meaning of his own life. To do this is to immeasurably exaggerate the significance of some necessarily particular and limited and essentially always impotent human work. Indeed, it is, in a cowardly and unreflecting manner, to hide from the consciousness of the meaninglessness of life, to submerge this consciousness in the vanity of essentially just as meaningless cares and concerns. Whether a man concerns himself with riches, glory, love, or with getting his daily bread; or whether he concerns himself with the happiness and salvation of all of mankind — his life is meaningless in both cases. In the latter case, however, to the general meaninglessness there is added a false illusion, an artificial self-deception. In order to *seek* the meaning of life — let alone find it — one must first stop what one is doing, concentrate one's mental faculties, and stop "concerning" oneself with things. Contrary to the general view, *not doing anything* is truly more important here than the most important and philanthropic work, for freedom from all human work is the first (although far from sufficient) condition for seeking the meaning of life.

Thus we see that to replace the question of the meaning of life with the question "What is to be done in order to save the world and thereby to give meaning to one's life?" is to replace the primary search for the unshakable ground of one's life, a search rooted in the very essence of man, by a striving, based on pride and illusion, to remake life and to give it meaning by one's own human powers. The fundamental, perplexing, and agonizing question of this tendency — "When will the real day arrive, the day of the triumph of truth and reason on earth, the day when all earthly disorder, chaos, and meaninglessness will disappear?" — this question receives the same sober, calm, and rational answer both from sober life-wisdom, which looks directly at the world and has a precise understanding of its empirical nature, and from the profound religious consciousness, which understands that the spiritual depths of being cannot be encompassed within the limits of empirical earthly life. This answer, overcoming the immature dreaminess and romanticism of the question itself, can only be as follows: "Within the limits of *this* world, before the yearned-for supramundane transfiguration of the latter, it will *never* arrive."

Whatever man might accomplish, whatever technological, social, and intellectual improvements he might introduce into his life, tomorrow and the day after tomorrow will *not differ* in any fundamental way from yesterday and today in the face of the question of the meaning of life. This world will always be ruled by meaningless chance, where man is an impotent leaf of grass which can be destroyed by the heat of the sun or the storms of earth. His life, always brief and fragmentary, will never contain the yearned-for spiritual fullness which gives meaning to life. And evil, stupidity, and blind passion will always rule on earth. And the question "What is to be done in order to terminate this state, in order to remake the world for the better?" will receive the same calm and rational answer: "Nothing can be done, for such a task surpasses human powers."

When one fully and clearly understands the obviousness of this answer, the very question "What is to be done?" acquires a new meaning, one that is legitimate. It comes to mean not "How can I remake the world in order to save it?" but *"How should I myself live* in order not to drown and perish in this chaos of life?" In other words, the only religiously grounded and non-illusory statement of the question "What is to be done?" consists not in the question "How can I save the world?" but in the question "How can I participate in the principle which alone can assure the salvation of the world?"

It is worthy of attention that, in the Gospels, the question "What is to be done?" is repeatedly posed in such terms. And the answers given to this question constantly underscore that the "doing," the work, which can lead to the desired goal here does not have anything in common with any external activity, with any external human works, but consists entirely in the work of inner regeneration through self-renunciation, repentance, and faith. Thus, in the Acts of the Apostles, we learn that, in Jerusalem, on the day of the Pentecost, the Jews, having heard the apostle Peter's divinely inspired discourse, "said unto Peter and to the rest of the apostles, 'Men and brethren, what shall we do?'" This is what Peter told them: "Repent, and be baptized every one of you in the name of Jesus Christ for the remission of sins, and ye shall receive the gift of the Holy Spirit" (Acts 2:37-38). Repentance and baptism and — as their fruit — the acquisition of the gift of the Holy Spirit are indicated here as the only necessary human work. We learn from the following passage that this work truly attained its goal and saved those who accomplished it: "Then they that gladly received his word were baptized. . . . And they continued stedfastly in the apostles' doctrine and fellowship, and in breaking of bread, and in prayers. . . . And all that believed were together, and had all things common. . . . And they, continuing daily with one accord in the temple, and breaking bread from house to house, did eat their meat with gladness and singleness of heart, praising God, and having favor with all the people" (2:41-47).

Similarly, when the Savior Himself was asked, "What shall we do, that we might work the works of God?" He answered, "This is the work of God, that ye believe on him whom he hath sent" (John 6:28-29). Likewise, when the lawyer posed the tempting question "What shall I do to inherit eternal life?" Christ answered by reminding him of the two eternal commandments, that of the love for God and that of the love for one's neighbor: "This do, and thou shalt live" (Luke 10:25-28). Love for God with all your heart, with all your soul, with all your strength, and with all your mind, and the love for one's neighbor that is based on the love for God — this is the sole "work" that is salvific for life.

The rich young man asks Christ the same question — "What shall I do that I may inherit eternal life?" — and Christ, after first mentioning the commandments that forbid evil deeds and command love for one's neighbor, says, "One thing thou lackest: go thy way, sell whatsoever thou hast, and give to the poor, and thou shalt have treasure in heaven: and come, take up the cross, and follow me" (Mark 10:17-21; cf. Matt. 19:16-21). It is permissible to think that the rich young man "went away sorrowful" not only because "he had great possessions" (Matt. 19:22; cf. Mark 10:22), but also because he had hoped to receive instructions about a "work" which he could accomplish himself, by his own powers, and perhaps by means of his possessions; and that he was disappointed when he learned that the only "work" commanded him was to have treasure in heaven and to follow Christ. In any case, here too the Word of God impressively notes the vanity of all human works and indicates that self-renunciation and faith are the only things that are truly necessary and salvific for man.

Thus, "What is to be done?" can legitimately mean only one thing: "How can I live in such a way that I will illuminate my life with meaning and thus give it an unshakable foundation?" In other words, it is not through some particular human work that the meaninglessness of life is overcome and that meaning is given to it; rather, *the sole human work consists only in seeking and finding the meaning of life,* apart from all particular, earthly works. But where can it be sought, and how can one find it?

· III ·

The Conditions for the Possibility
of the Meaning of Life

L et us first inquire into the meaning of the phrase "to find the meaning of life." More precisely, let us ask, *What* exactly are we seeking?
What do we mean by the notion "the meaning of life"? Under *what* conditions would we consider its meaning to be found?

We take "meaning" here to be roughly equivalent to "rationality." Relatively speaking, we call "rational" all that which is purposive, which leads
directly to a goal or helps to attain the latter. That behavior is rational
which accords with a prescribed goal and leads to its attainment: we call
rational or meaningful the use of a means which helps us to attain a prescribed goal. But all this is only relatively rational — precisely given the
condition that the goal itself is indisputably rational or meaningful. For example, we can call relatively "rational" the behavior of a man who is capable of adapting to life, of earning money, of making a career for himself —
but this assumes that success in life, riches, a high social position, and so
on are recognized by us as indisputable and in this sense "rational" goods.

But if, having become disillusioned by life, having recognized its
"meaninglessness" (if only because of the briefness and instability of all
of its goods or because they do not give true satisfaction to our soul), we
recognize as dubious the very goal of such strivings, that behavior which
is relatively — i.e., in relation to *its* goal — rational and meaningful will
then appear to us as irrational and meaningless in the absolute sense.
That is exactly how it is with regard to the predominant content of ordinary human life. We see that the majority of people devote the greater

26

part of their powers and time to a series of entirely purposive actions, that they are constantly preoccupied with the attainment of certain goals and that they act correctly in order to attain them; that is, in the majority of cases, they act fully "rationally." But, at the same time, since either the goals themselves are "meaningless" or, at the very least, the question of their "meaningfulness" remains undecided and disputable, all of human life takes on the character of a meaningless going in circles, the way a squirrel goes round in a wheel; it takes on the character of a set of meaningless actions which — unexpectedly, without any connection with these goals which are set by man, and therefore also completely meaninglessly — are interrupted by death.

Consequently, the condition for the genuine — and not only relative — rationality of life is not only that it rationally accomplish certain goals but also that these goals themselves be rational.

But what do we mean by a "rational goal"? A means is rational when it leads to a goal. But a goal — if it is a genuine and ultimate goal, and not just a means to something else — does not lead to anything and therefore cannot be assessed from the point of view of its purposiveness. It must be intrinsically rational, rational as such. But what does this mean, and how is this possible? This difficulty — which is transformed into an absolute unresolvability — serves as the basis of a sophism which is often used to prove that life is necessarily meaningless or that the very question of the meaning of life is illegitimate. It is argued that every action is meaningful when it serves a goal; but life as a whole does not have any goal outside itself: "Life is given to me for the sake of life."[1] Therefore, either one must reconcile oneself, once and for all, with the fatal "meaninglessness" of life deriving from the logic of things; or — and this is more correct — one must recognize that the very posing of the question of the meaning of life is illegitimate — that this question is one of those which cannot be resolved because of their internal absurdity. The question of the "meaning" of something always has a relative significance; it presupposes "meaning" for something, purposiveness with regard to the attainment of a definite goal. But life as a whole does not have any goal, and therefore the question of its "meaning" cannot be posed.

---

1. The source of this quotation has not been identified. *Trans.*

However convincing this argument might seem at first glance, our heart protests instinctively against it: We feel that the question of the meaning of life is, in and of itself, by no means a meaningless question and that, however painful for us might be the consideration that it is unresolved or unresolvable, we are not consoled by the argument that the very posing of the question is illegitimate. For a moment we can evade this question, chase it away from ourselves, but the next moment it is posed not by "us" and not by our "mind," but it itself is inexorably present before us; and our soul, often in deathly torment, inquires, "What is one to live for?"

It is evident that our life, the simple elemental process of living, of being in the world, and of being conscious of this fact, cannot by any means be a goal in itself for us. It cannot be such a goal first of all because, in general, the sufferings and pains of life predominate over its joys and pleasures, and despite the power of the animal instinct of self-preservation, we are often uncertain why we must pull this heavy weight. But even independent of this fact, life cannot be our goal in itself because, in its essence, it is not an immobile abiding in itself, a self-sufficient repose; rather, life is the doing of something or the striving for something. Moments in which we are free of all activity or striving are felt by us as an excruciatingly painful state of emptiness and dissatisfaction. We cannot live for life; like it or not, we always live for something. However, in the majority of cases, this "something," being a goal toward which we strive, in its content is in turn a means, and moreover a means for the preservation of life. This leads to an excruciating vicious circle which makes us feel most acutely the meaninglessness of life and produces in us a painful yearning to find its meaning: We live in order to toil over something, to strive for something, but we toil, take care of things, and strive — in order to live. And made weary by this circling in the squirrel's wheel, we seek the "meaning of life": We seek a striving and a work which is not directed at a mere preservation of life. And we seek a life which is not consumed by the strenuous labor of its preservation.

We return by this path to the question posed above. Our life acquires meaning when it serves some rational goal whose content cannot be merely this empirical life itself. But wherein lies this content, and first of all under what conditions can we recognize the ultimate goal as "rational"?

If the rationality of this goal does not consist in the fact that it is a means to something else (otherwise, it would not be a genuine, ultimate goal), then it can consist only in the fact that this goal is an indisputable, self-sufficient value about which it is meaningless to pose the question "For what purpose?" In order to be meaningful, our life — contrary to the assurances of the adherents of "life for life's sake" and in agreement with the explicit demands of our soul — *must serve the supreme and absolute good.*

But that is not all. We have seen that, in the sphere of relative "rationality," one often encounters cases when something is meaningful from the point of view of a third person, but not for oneself. (Recall the above-mentioned example of slave labor, which is meaningful for the slave owner but not for the slave himself.) The same thing is conceivable in the sphere of absolute rationality. If our life were given to the service of a supreme and absolute good, but a good which is not a good for us or one in which we ourselves do not participate, in this case our life would nevertheless remain meaningless *for us.* We have already remarked on the meaninglessness of a life devoted to the good of future generations; but here we can add that this meaninglessness is determined by the relativity, limitedness, or uncertainty of the goal itself. Let us take, for example, Hegel's philosophical ethics. In the latter, human life must acquire meaning as a manifestation and instrument of the self-development and self-knowledge of the absolute spirit; but the moral difficulties which this theory encounters are very well known. When our own Belinsky,[2] after having become familiar with Hegel's philosophy, indignantly exclaimed, "So, it turns out that I gain knowledge and live *not for myself*[3] but for the development of some absolute spirit. Why should I toil for this spirit?" — he was of course absolutely right in essence. Life gains meaning when, serving the absolute and supreme good, it is at the same time not a diminution but an affirmation and enrichment of itself; it gains meaning when it serves the absolute good, which is also a good for me. Or, in other words, only one good can be recognized as absolute in the sense of

2. Vissarion Belinsky (1811-1848), Russian literary critic, was an early leader of the Russian intelligentsia and a major representative of German absolute idealism, as well as of the subsequent reaction against it, in nineteenth-century Russian philosophy. *Trans.*

3. The italics are Frank's. *Trans.*

perfect certainty: a good which is both a *self-sufficient good,* surpassing all of my personal interests, and a *good for me.* It must be a good both in the objective and in the subjective sense: it must be both a supreme value which we seek for its own sake and a value fulfilling and enriching me myself.

But how can this double condition be realized, and does it not contain an internal contradiction? By a good in the objective sense we mean a self-sufficient value or goal which does not serve anything else and the striving toward which is justified precisely by its inner worth. By a good in the subjective sense we mean, on the contrary, something pleasant, necessary, or useful *for us,* that is, something of service in relation to us ourselves and our subjective needs, and thus clearly having the significance not of a supreme goal but of a means for our well-being. It is clear, however, that if we can find satisfaction only in a good combining these heterogeneous and apparently contradictory features, we mean by it something at least conceivable and in this sense possible. When we dream of such a good, when we concretely imagine it, this abstract contradiction does not by any means bother us, and we do not notice it at all; evidently, the error is contained in the abstract definitions themselves with which we have approached the clarification of this concept. Self-sufficient good alone — good in the objective sense — does not satisfy us; service of even an absolute principle, but one in which I myself do not participate and which does not adorn and warm my personal life, cannot give meaning to the latter. But neither does good in the subjective sense alone — subjective pleasure, joy, happiness — give meaning to my life, for, as we see, every life, even the happiest, is poisoned by the torment of the question "For what purpose?" It does not have meaning in itself.

That which we are seeking as the true condition of a meaningful life must therefore combine these two principles in such a way that they are *extinguished* in it as *separate* principles, and only *their unity* is given. We are seeking neither one or another subjective life, however happy it might be, nor a cold, lifeless, objective good, however perfect it might be in itself. Rather, we are seeking that which can be called the satisfaction or "filling" of our soul's emptiness and anguished yearning. We are seeking meaningful, objectively full, *self-sufficiently valuable life.* That is why no separate, abstractly definable good, whether it be beauty, truth, harmony, or something of that sort, can satisfy us; for then life, life itself as a whole, and first of all our own life, would remain on the sidelines, as it were, would not be wholly embraced and permeated by this good, but would only serve it externally, as a means. But, after all, what we yearn to make meaningful is our own personal life. Nor are we seeking subjective pleasures, for we are conscious of their meaninglessness. What we are seeking is the meaningful fullness of life; we are seeking a state of blissful fulfillment, which in itself is the supreme and indisputable value.

Consequently, the supreme good cannot be anything else than *life* itself; however, this is not life as a meaningless process of flux and eternal movement toward something other, but life as *the eternal repose of bliss,* as the self-knowing and self-experiencing fullness of self-fulfillment. This constitutes the obvious grain of truth (a truth, however, that is poorly understood and ineptly expressed) contained in the assertion that life is its own goal and does not have a goal outside of itself. Our empirical life, brief and fragmentary, besieged by inevitable troubles and needs, marked by a striving toward something outside of it — our empirical life is clearly not a goal in itself, and cannot be such a goal. On the contrary, as we have seen, the first condition for the meaningfulness of life is that we stop our meaningless chase after life itself, that we stop the meaningless expenditure of life for the sake of life itself, and that, instead, we make our life serve something higher, something which has its justification in itself. But this higher thing must, in turn, be life — a life into which our life will pour and by which it will be wholly permeated. *Life in the good,* or *the good life,* or *the good as life* — that is the goal of our strivings. And the absolute opposite of every rational life-goal is death, non-being. The sought-for good cannot be only an "ideal," something immaterial and concretely non-existent; it must be a living being which embraces our life and gives the latter ultimate fulfillment precisely because it is the expression of the ultimate and deepest essence of our life.

We have a concrete example (and more than an example) of such a good in *love.* When we love with a true love, what do we seek in it and what satisfies us in it? Do we only desire to taste personal delight from love, to use the loved being and our relation to the latter as a means to our subjective pleasures? That would be debauchery, not true love; and such a relation would first of all be punished by the emptiness of soul, coldness, and anguish of unfulfillment we would feel. Do we desire to give our life to the service of the loved being? Of course we do, but not in such a way that this service would make our life empty and weary. We desire to serve the loved being; we are ready for self-sacrifice, even for death, for the sake of the loved being, but this is precisely because this service, this self-sacrifice and death, is not only joyous for us but also imparts to our life fullness and the peace of satisfaction. Love is not a cold, empty, egotistical hunger for pleasure; nor is it a slave's service, the annihilation of oneself for the sake of another. Love is an overcoming of our selfish personal life, an overcoming which gives us the blissful fullness of *true life* and thereby gives meaning to our life. The concepts of "objective" good and "subjective" good are both insufficient here for expressing the good of love. This good is higher than either concept; it is the good of *life* achieved by overcoming the opposition between "mine" and "another's," between the subjective and the objective.

However, love for an earthly, human being does not, in and of itself, give true and ultimate meaning to life. If both the loving one and the beloved one are seized by the current of time, are thrown into the meaningless vortex of life, are limited in time, then in such a love it is possible to forget oneself temporarily, it is possible to have a reflection and an illusory foretaste of true life and its meaning; but it is not possible to attain the ultimate fulfillment which gives meaning to life. It is clear that the supreme, absolute good which fills our life must be *eternal*. For as soon as we conceive of this absolute good in terms of some temporal state of the life of man or the life of the world, there arises the question of its proper meaning. No temporal thing, no thing that has a beginning and an end, can be a goal in itself, can be conceived as something self-sufficient: Either it is necessary for something else and thus has meaning as a means, or it is meaningless. The flux of time, this variegated and vertiginous cinematographic succession of pictures of life, this appearance of things from some unknown place and their disappearance to some unknown place, this possession of things by the agitation and instability of continuous movement — this flux of time imparts a quality of "vanity" to everything in the world, makes it meaningless. Time itself is, as it were, an expression of the meaninglessness of the world. The objectively full and grounded life sought by us cannot be this agitation, this meaningless transition from one thing to another, this inner unfulfillment which is, as it were, the essence of the flux of the world in time.

The life sought by us must be *eternal life*. That absolute good the service of which gives meaning to our life must first of all be eternal: it must be unshakably grounded in itself and rise above all temporal instability. However, it must be eternal not only *for itself*, but also *for me*. If it is for me *only* a goal which I will attain or seek to attain in the future, then the entire past and present of my life, since they are separated from the future, are thus not justified and not meaningful. It must instead be a goal which at the same time, as we have seen, is *the abiding ground of my entire life*. I seek this goal not as a remote and extraneous object which is alien to my "I," but as a principle implanted in my very depths; and only in such a case is my life warmed and illuminated with "meaning" by it from beginning to end.

But even this is not enough. Since my life nonetheless has a beginning and an end, and exhausts itself in this brief duration, this eternal good remains unattainable for my life, for it is unattainable precisely *because of its eternity*. It is true that I can grasp this eternal good with my thought, but I can also grasp with my thought much that is extraneous and alien to me. And if possession in thought were the same as genuine possession, then all people would be rich and happy. No, I must *genuinely* possess this eternal good, and I must possess it precisely *in eternity*. Otherwise, my life would be deprived of meaning as before; I would not be a participant in the higher good which gives meaning, but would at best only fleetingly touch it. But, after all, *my personal life* must have a meaning: not being a goal in itself, in its ultimate depths it must nevertheless not only strive for and use the good, but it must become fused with the good, become *the good itself*. Infinitely surpassing my limited empirical personality and the brief temporal duration of the latter's life, being an eternal, all-embracing, and all-illuminating principle, the eternal good must at the same time *belong to me*; and I must possess it, and not only seek it or touch it. Consequently, in another sense, as we have already pointed out, the eternal good must be identical with my life — not with its empirical, temporal, and limited nature, but with its ultimate depth and essence. The living good, or the good as life, must be *eternal* life; and this eternal life must be my personal life. My life can acquire meaning only if it possesses *eternity.*

Reflecting upon this more deeply, we remark the necessity of an additional condition for the meaningfulness of life. Not only must I serve the eternal good in a *de facto* way and, abiding in it and permeating my life with it, thereby acquire true life, but I must also continuously be rationally conscious of this whole relation. For if I unconsciously participate in this service and it only enriches me unconsciously for me, then as before I am *conscious* of my life as abiding in the obscurity of meaninglessness; as before I do not have the *consciousness* of a meaningful life; but the very meaningfulness of life is impossible without this consciousness. Furthermore, this consciousness must not be accidental; it must not approach from outside, as it were, its content of a "meaningful life" and be a principle external to this content.

Our consciousness, our "mind," that principle in us by virtue of which we "know" something, demands, as it were, a metaphysical foundation, a rootedness in the ultimate depths of being. We genuinely possess a "meaningful life" not when *we* are "conscious" — somehow from outside, by virtue of our own human initiative and our own efforts — of this life, but only when this life itself is conscious of itself in us. The peace and self-groundedness of the ultimate attainment are possible only in our full and perfect unity with the absolute good and perfect life; and this unity exists only where we are not only warmed and enriched but also *illuminated* by the perfection. Consequently, not only must this good objectively *be* true, and not only must it be perceived by *me* as true (for in the latter case one cannot exclude the possibility of doubting it and of forgetting it), but it itself must be Truth itself, the very light of knowledge which illuminates me. The full significance of what we call "the meaning of life" and of what we yearn for as such meaning is by no means exhausted by "rationality" in the sense of purposiveness or absolute value. This full significance also includes rationality in the sense of "attained meaning" or *attainment* as *the light of knowledge* which illuminates us. Meaninglessness is darkness and blindness; "meaning" is light and clarity, and meaningfulness is the total suffusion of life by clear, peaceful, all-illuminating light. The good, perfect life, fullness and the peace of fulfillment, and the light of truth are all *one and the same thing* and constitute the "meaning of life." In the "meaning of life" we seek an absolutely firm foundation, genuinely satisfying nourishment, as well as the illumination of our life. This unbreakable unity of perfect fulfillment and perfect clarity, this unity of life and Truth, is what constitutes the sought-for "meaning of life."

Thus, life becomes meaningful to the extent that it freely and consciously serves the absolute and supreme good. This good is eternal *life,* quickening human life and serving as the eternal foundation and true fulfillment of the latter; and it is also absolute truth, the light of reason, permeating and illuminating human life. Our life attains meaning to the extent that it is a rational path to a goal, or a path to the rational supreme goal; otherwise, it is a meaningless and errant wandering. But such a true path for our life can only be that which at the same time is both life and Truth: "I am the way, the truth, and the life" (John 14:6).

We can now briefly sum up our reflections. If life is to have a meaning, two conditions are necessary: first, *the existence of God;* and second, our own communion with God, the possibility that we might attain *life in God* or *divine life.* What is necessary, first of all, is that, despite all the meaninglessness of the world's life, there exists the general condition of its meaningfulness. What is needed is that the ultimate, supreme, absolute foundation of the world's life be not blind chance, not the chaotic and confused flux of time (ejecting everything out of itself for an instant and then sucking it back in), not the darkness of ignorance — but God, as the eternal foundation, as eternal life, as absolute good, as the all-embracing light of reason.

And second, what is necessary is that we ourselves — despite all our impotence, despite the blindness and destructiveness of our passions, despite the random character and brief duration of our lives — be not only "creatures" of God, not only clay pots molded by the potter as he wants, and even not only "slaves" of God, fulfilling His will submissively and only for Him, but also free participants in the divine life itself, in such a way that, in serving Him, we do not negate our own lives, but instead affirm, enrich, and illuminate them. This service must be a true daily bread, and a true water, satisfying us. Furthermore, we can acquire the meaning of life *for our own selves* only if, in serving God, we, as the sons and heirs of the master of the house, serve in our own work; we can acquire this meaning only if His life, light, eternity, and bliss can also become ours; only if our lives can become divine, and we ourselves can become "gods," can be "deified."[4] We must have the possibility of overcoming death, which deprives all things of meaning, of overcoming the blindness and fierce agitation of our blind passions, of overcoming all the blind and evil powers of the meaningless life of the world, which crush or enslave us — in order to find this true life-path, which is for us both true Life and the genuine living Truth.

But how can we find this path which coincides with truth and life? How can we become sure of the genuineness of God's existence and of the possibility that we can genuinely find divinity, that we can participate in eternal bliss? It is easy to state such ideas, but is it possible to realize them? Do they not contradict our entire immediate life-experience? Are they not a dream which is found to be unrealizable as soon as it is expressed?

We are confronted by the most difficult of problems, and we must not evade its difficulties in a cowardly manner. If man is to attain the meaning of life, he must find the absolute, supreme goal, but are not all conceivable goods relative? Man must possess the truth itself and eternal life, but is he not fated always to err, or merely to seek the truth, or in the best case to find particular and imperfect truths, not the Truth itself? And is eternal life not a dreamily utopian concept, unrealizable in its very meaning? It is easy to talk about and to preach about "eternal life," but what meaning does it have when one is confronted, in one's actual life, by the pitiless and inexorable fact of the fatal briefness of one's own life, of the lives of those we love, and in general of the life of all that lives and moves in the world? One's dreams are dispersed like smoke; one's words are exposed as hypocritical and sentimental "words, only words" in the face of the terrible logic of death, in the face of the lamentation over the body of a dear deceased, in the face of the corruptibility, destruction, and meaningless disappearance of all living things in the world. And where is one to find, and how is one to prove, God's existence and reconcile with it one's own life and the world's life as a whole — in the face of the evil, suffering, blindness, and meaninglessness that

---

4. Frank is referring to the patristic doctrine of "deification" or "theosis." *Trans.*

wholly dominate and permeate the world's life? Apparently, there are only two choices here: either, honestly and courageously, to look directly at the facts of life as it actually is; or, hiding from these facts in a cowardly manner, to surrender to dreams of life as it should be if it is to have meaning. But why do we need such powerless dreams, and what value do they have? The hope of seeing one's dream realized, of recognizing the truth in it — is this not merely a self-deception of cowardly souls who console themselves with falsehood in order not to perish from horror in the face of the truth?

We should not and cannot push these doubts away from ourselves; we are obligated to take upon ourselves the entire burden of honest and bitter truth contained in them. But neither should we, in an untimely manner, fall into despair. However little progress we have made so far in resolving the question of the meaning of life, we have at least achieved one thing: we have gained knowledge of what we mean when we speak of the meaning of life, and of the conditions under which we would consider this meaning realized. Let us now, without succumbing to any illusions or retreating before the greatest difficulties, but uniting the fearlessness of honest thought with the fearlessness of will which strives to attain the unique goal of our life — let us now reflect upon to what degree these conditions are realizable or given, and in what form they are realizable or given.

IV

The Meaninglessness of Life

That life, as it actually is, is meaningless; that it does not in the slightest satisfy the conditions under which it could be recognized as having meaning — this is a truth attested to by personal experience, by direct observation of life, by historical knowledge of mankind's fate, and by natural-scientific knowledge of the structure and evolution of the world.

Meaningless first of all (and this is the most important thing from the point of view of personal spiritual needs) is the personal life of each of us. The first minimal (so to speak) condition for the possibility of attaining the meaning of life is *freedom;* only if we are free can we act "meaningfully," strive toward a rational goal, seek fulfillment. But on all sides we are constrained, enchained by the forces of necessity. We are corporeal and are therefore subject to all the blind, mechanical laws of cosmic matter; when we stumble, we fall like a stone, and if by chance this happens on railroad tracks or in front of a speeding car, the elementary laws of physics will immediately terminate our life and, with it, all our hopes, aspirations, and plans for the rational realization of life. A tiny bacillus of tuberculosis or of some other disease can terminate the life of a genius, can stop the most profound thought and the most sublime aspirations. We are also subject to the blind laws and forces of organic life: because of the inexorable action of these forces, even the normal term of our lives is too short for the full manifestation and realization of the spiritual powers implanted in us. Just as we begin to learn from our own experience of

life and from the store of knowledge accumulated before us to live rationally and to correctly realize our vocation — we find that our body has
deteriorated and that we are approaching the grave. This produces in us
the tragic sense — inevitable even in the case of a long life — of the un-
timeliness and unexpectedness of death ("What? Is it already the end!
How can this be? I have just begun to truly live, to correct the errors of
the past, to redeem time spent uselessly and powers squandered in
vain!") as well as disbelief that we are aging.

Moreover, we are also inwardly burdened by the heavy weight of
blind, elemental biological forces, hindering our rational life. From our
parents we inherit passions and vices which torment us and on which
we fruitlessly expend our powers; in our own animal nature we are condemned to suffering and hard labor, and meaninglessly suffer punishment for the sins of our fathers or in general for sins to which nature itself has condemned us. Our best and most rational aspirations are either
smashed against external obstacles or are rendered impotent by our own
blind passions. Furthermore, blind nature has organized us in such a way
that we are condemned to illusions, to wander into a dead end; and we
discover the illusoriness and erroneousness of our desires only after they
have done us irreparable harm and all our best efforts have led to nothing. One man will waste himself on pleasures and debauchery, but after
his physical and spiritual health have been hopelessly shattered, he will
in his anguish become convinced of the vulgarity and meaninglessness
of all pleasures: they cannot take away the anguish of his life. Another
man will ascetically abstain from all of life's pleasures, hardening himself
and saving himself for a great vocation or holy work, but when his life begins to incline toward its end, he will become convinced that he never
had a vocation and that his work was not at all holy; and in fruitless repentance he will lament the fact that he never tasted the pleasures of life.
There are those who remain alone, afraid of burdening themselves with
the hardships of family; they suffer from the coldness of solitary old age
and lament the fact that the comfort of family and the caresses of love
can no longer be attained. And there are those who, having succumbed
to the temptation of having a family, turn out to be burdened by family
cares and immersed in the petty vortex of family quarrels and worries;
they fruitlessly repent that they voluntarily gave up their freedom for

imaginary goods, sold themselves into slavery, and did not realize their true vocation. All our passions and most powerful desires deceptively pretend to be something absolutely important and precious for us, promise us joy and peace if we are successful in satisfying them; but later on, retrospectively, when it is too late to correct the error, all of these passions and desires reveal their illusoriness, the falseness of their pretension to exhaust the most profound aspiration of our being and, through their satisfaction, to give fullness and stability to our existence.

This produces the melancholy, profoundly and inexorably tragic consciousness, inevitable for all people, expressed by the French saying *"Si jeunesse savait, si vieillesse pouvait."*[1] This is the consciousness of deceived hopes, of the unattainability of true happiness on earth. Goethe, who was called "the favorite of fortune" and lived an exceptionally long, happy, and productive life, who possessed the rarest of gifts, the ability to combine creative energy, immense diligence in work, and a mighty self-restraining power of the will with the desire and the capacity to experience all of life's pleasures, to drink in all the joys of life — this chosen one of mankind confessed, at the end of his life, that in the course of his eighty years he had known only a few days of complete happiness and satisfaction. And he personally experienced all the inevitable tragedy of human life; he attested that the essence of life is known only by those who eat their bread with tears and who pass sleepless, tormented nights in anguish and lamentation; and that fate consoles us only with one unceasing refrain: "Suffer deprivations" (*"Entbehren sollst du, sollst ent-behren"*[2]). If that is the life wisdom of "the favorite of fortune," then what is the sum total of their lives that must be added up by all other men, who are less successful and less gifted, with all their powerlessness, with the heavy weight of their destiny, with all of their inwardly rending contradictions and the spiritual weaknesses which obscure their paths?

All of us are slaves of blind fate, of the blind forces of fate both outside us and inside us. And a slave, as we already know and as is self-evident, cannot have a meaningful life. The ancient Greeks, who had such an acute sense of the cosmic order, of the harmony of the world's life, also

---

1. "If youth only knew, if age only could." *Trans.*
2. "Thou shalt abstain, thou shalt abstain" (from *Faust*, I, 4). *Trans.*

bequeathed to us eternal, unforgettable examples of the tragic consciousness that there is no place for human dreams and hopes in this harmony. The popular consciousness believed that the gods are envious of human happiness and always take measures to punish and humiliate the happy man, to take revenge on accidental human success by the bitter blows of fate. And on the other hand this consciousness also believed that even the blissful gods were subject, as to a higher principle, to pitiless blind fate. The more purified religious consciousness of the Greek sages taught that, in accordance with the laws of world harmony, no man should grasp too much for himself, no man should exceed by too much the common level, but that, instead, every man should know his modest place and that even man's *individuality* is a sinful illusion, punished by death. Only by voluntarily recognizing himself as a dependent and serviceable cog in the cosmic whole, only by humbly accepting his slavish dependence on the cosmos and his cosmic insignificance, does man subordinate himself to the divine will and fulfill his sole vocation. Only by accepting this dependence can he hope to keep from ruining himself. The two views have the same result. And thus the naïve Homer says,

> In truth, of all the creatures that breathe and crawl in the dust,
> None on the whole earth is more wretched than man.[3]

And all the Greek poets harmoniously repeat this refrain: "The land and the sea are both full of woes for man" (Hesiod). "Weak is man's life, fruitless his work; in his brief life, sorrow follows sorrow" (Simonides). In this cosmic whole, man is only "a wind and a shadow" or even "the dream of a shadow" (Pindar). And all of ancient philosophy, from Anaximander, Heraclitus, and Empedocles to Plato, Marcus Aurelius, and Plotinus — even though in all else it diverges from and opposes the teachings of the poets — all of ancient philosophy is in agreement with Greek poetry in this pessimism, in this bitter recognition of the hopeless vanity, infirmity, and meaninglessness of man's earthly life. In agreement with ancient

---

3. *Odyssey*, Book XVIII, 22. The verses here are translated from the Russian version used by Frank. *Trans.*

philosophy is the entire life wisdom of the rest of mankind, of the Bible and the Mahabharata, of the Babylonian epos, and of the gravestone inscriptions of ancient Egypt.

> Vanity of vanities, saith the Preacher, vanity of vanities; all is vanity. What profit hath a man of all his labor which he taketh under the sun? . . . That which befalleth the sons of men befalleth beasts; even one thing befalleth them: as the one dieth, so dieth the other; yea, they have all one breath; so that a man hath no pre-eminence above a beast: for all is vanity. . . . I praised the dead which are already dead more than the living which are yet alive. Yea, better is he than both they, which hath not yet been, who hath not seen the evil work that is done under the sun. . . . I returned, and saw under the sun that the race is not to the swift, nor the battle to the strong, neither yet bread to the wise, nor yet riches to men of understanding, nor yet favor to men of skill; but time and chance happeneth to them all. (Eccles. 1:2-3; 3:19; 4:2-3; 9:11)

But let us even assume that the wisdom of all times and nations is not right. Let us assume that it is possible to have a genuinely happy life, that all our desires will be satisfied, that the goblet of life will be full of sweet wine for us and not poisoned by any bitterness. Nevertheless, life, even the sweetest and most peaceful life, cannot, in itself, satisfy us. The unavoidable question "For what purpose?" produces in us an insatiable sadness even when we are happy. Life for the sake of the process of life itself does not satisfy us, but only puts us to sleep for a while. Inevitable death, terminating both the happiest life and the unhappiest life, makes both of them equally meaningless. Our empirical life is a fragment: In and for itself, without connection to some whole, our empirical life can have as little meaning as the fragment of a page torn out of a book. If our empirical life can have meaning, this is only in connection with the general life of mankind and of the entire world. And we have already seen that a meaningful life must inevitably be at the service of something other than it itself as a self-enclosed personal life, that only by fulfilling a vocation, only by actualizing some suprapersonal and self-sufficient value, can man find himself as a rational being, requiring a rational, meaningful life. The most proximate whole with which we are connected and a part of which we constitute is the life of a nation or of mankind; outside of our homeland and a connection with its destiny, outside of cultural creativity, outside of a creative unity with the past and the future of mankind, outside of love for and solidarity with people, outside of participation in their common destiny, we cannot actualize ourselves, we cannot acquire a genuinely meaningful life. Like the leaf or branch of a tree, we are nourished by the juices of the whole; we blossom by the life of the whole, and dry up and fall apart into dust if there is no life in the whole itself. For the individual life to have meaning, it is necessary that human life in general have meaning, that the history of mankind be a coherent and meaningful process in which some great common and indisputably valuable goal is being achieved. But here too, if we dispassionately and honestly examine the empirical course of things, we will find a new disillusionment, a new obstacle to the possibility of finding the meaning of life.

For the common life of mankind is just as meaningless as every individual human life. The history of mankind, if we seek its immanent and inherent meaning, deceives our expectations to the same extent as our personal life. On the one hand, this history is a collection of meaningless accidents, a long line of collective, national, and international events which do not follow rationally the one from the other, which do not lead to any goal, but which merely happen as the result of the elemental collision and intersection of collective human passions. And on the other hand, insofar as history nevertheless represents the successive actualization of human ideals, it also represents the collapse of these ideals, the inexorable exposure of their illusoriness and insolvency, an infinitely long and excruciating object-lesson through which mankind learns to perceive the vanity of its hopes for the rational and good organization of its collective life. Faith in progress, in the unceasing and continuous improvement of mankind, in mankind's constant ascent — without pauses and falls — to the height of goodness and reason — this faith, which in the course of the last two centuries inspired a multitude of people, at the present time is exposed as so obviously groundless that we can only wonder at the naïvete of the generations that held it.

In its empirical historical life, mankind does not by any means move

43

"forward." Insofar as we seek to ground our life upon the service of the social good, the realization of a perfect social order, the embodiment of the principles of justice, goodness, and reason in the collective life and relations of man — insofar as we seek this, we must with sober courage admit that the world's history does not by any means represent an approach to this goal, that at the present time mankind is no closer to this goal than it was one century, two centuries, or twenty centuries ago. Even the preservation of the values it had attained has turned out to be impossible for mankind. Where today can we find the wisdom and beauty of the ancient Greeks, the mere memory of which fills our souls with a sad and tender love? Who of the present-day sages, unless he deludes himself with intellectual arrogance, can with his thought attain the spiritual heights where the thought of Plato or of Plotinus freely soared? Are we close today to the organization in peace and right of the entire cultural world under one authority which the world had attained in the golden era of the Roman Empire with its *pax Romana?* Can we hope for the rebirth in the world of those unattainable examples of profound and clear religious faith exhibited by the Christian martyrs and confessors of the first centuries of our era? Where can we find today the richness of the individuals, the blossoming fullness and diversity of the life of the Middle Ages, which the supercilious banality of the squalid "Enlightenment" called an epoch of barbarism and which, like an unrealizable dream, now beckons to itself all sensitive souls who are starving in the desert of contemporary civilization?

Truly, one must believe very strongly in the absolute value of external technological improvements — airplanes and wireless telegraphy, long-range ordnance and mustard gas, starched collars and water closets — if one is to share the faith in the continuous improvement of life. And is not the very progress of empirical science — undeniable over the past few centuries and beneficial in many ways — bought at the very high cost of that *spiritual* blindness, of that neglect of absolute values, of that vulgarity of bourgeois self-satisfaction which have had so many dispiriting successes in recent centuries and whose progress appears to be unceasing in the European world? And do we not see that Europe — highly cultured, enlightened, illuminated by scientific reason and purified by humanitarian moral ideas — entered on an inhuman and meaningless world war,[4] and now stands on the threshold of anarchy, savagery, and a new barbarism? And the horrifying historical catastrophe which occurred in our own homeland[5] and which stomped into the mud and handed over to the savage, unleashed mobs that which we honored in it as "Holy Russia" and that which we proudly dreamt of as "great Russia" — does this catastrophe not represent the decisive revelation and condemnation of the falseness of the "theory of progress"?

We have come to understand (and, here, immediate life-impressions coincide with the chief achievements of objective historical science over the past hundred years) that continuous progress does not exist, that mankind lives by a succession of ascents and falls, and that all of mankind's great achievements in all domains of life (governmental and social, scientific and artistic, religious and moral) come to an end and are replaced by periods of stagnation and decline, when mankind has to learn everything anew and once again rise from out of the depths. "All that is great on earth is dispersed like smoke — today it is Troy's turn, tomorrow it will be the turn of others."[6] Under the influence of this consciousness, one of the most subtle, sensitive, and universally educated historian-thinkers of our time — Oswald Spengler — teaches that universal history is essentially a meaningless succession of the birth, blossoming, decline, and death of individual cultures.

And when, dissatisfied with this conclusion, we seek behind this meaningless ebb and flow of the spiritual waves of historical life some coherence and logic; when we attempt to decode the rhythm of world history and, through it, its meaning, the only thing we achieve is to clarify the meaning of this history as a common human religious education through a series of bitter disappointments, exposing the vanity of all earthly human hopes and dreams. The history of mankind is the history of the successive collapse of mankind's hopes, empirically exposing its errors. All human ideals, all aspirations to build life on one or another separate moral principle, are weighed by life itself, found to be too light, and cast aside by life as unfit. Just as individual human life in its empiri-

---

4. Frank is referring to World War I. *Trans.*
5. Here Frank is referring to the Russian Revolution. *Trans.*
6. The source of this quotation has not been identified. *Trans.*

cal realization has only one meaning — to teach us the life wisdom that happiness is unrealizable, that all our dreams are illusory, and that the process of life is, as such, meaningless — so the life of humanity as a whole is an arduous school of experience, necessary to purge us of the illusion that happiness is possible for humanity as a whole, to expose the vanity and deceptiveness of all our hopes for the realization of the kingdom of goodness and justice in this world, the vanity of all our human plans of ideal social organization.

And how can it be otherwise? When we think of history, of the common fate of mankind, we tend to forget that the history of mankind is only a fragment, a dependent part of cosmic history, of the world's life, as a whole. The outer and inner enslavement by accidental and blind cosmic forces which are alien to our most cherished hopes, this enslavement — which we have perceived to be the fateful condition of the individual human life — is just as prevalent, if not more so, in the common life of mankind. Mankind is surrounded on all sides by the blind forces and fateful, blind necessities of cosmic nature. Just the fact that human life, both individual and collective, is to such a great degree reducible to that struggle for existence, that continuous, suicidal war for the means of nourishment which dominates the entire animal world — the fact that, despite all technological advances, the increasing population of mankind is causing relative deficits on earth of arable land, coal, iron, and everything else that people need, and that the struggle for the possession of these resources is becoming more intense and more embittered — just this fact of the increasingly acute struggle for existence attests sufficiently to what extent the elemental conditions of cosmic life constrain human life and infect it with their meaninglessness.

And in our souls — and precisely and especially in the soul of mankind as a collective whole, in the hearts of the national masses — there live passions and aspirations that are just as blind and murderous as all the other cosmic forces. And if an individual man can easily succumb to the self-deception that he is free of the blindness of the cosmic forces, it is precisely the national masses and all kinds of historical collectives which represent such striking examples of subordination to blind instincts and crude elemental passions that, in relation to them, self-deception is impossible or much less forgivable. Let us at least for a moment imagine with total realistic clarity the situation of mankind which corresponds to authentic reality, insofar as we are considering life in its empirical makeup: A clump of cosmic dirt called the Earth is hurtling through some corner of cosmic space; on its surface, hurtling along with it, there seethe billions and billions of living creatures, generated from the Earth itself, including two-legged creatures who call themselves human beings. Being meaninglessly hurtled through cosmic space, meaninglessly being born and dying in an instant in accordance with the laws of cosmic nature, at the same time, motivated by the same blind forces, they are fighting one another, are unceasingly striving toward something, are always busy with something, are always instituting among themselves certain rules and orders of life. And these insignificant creatures of nature are dreaming of the meaning of their common life; they desire to attain happiness, reason, and truth. What monstrous blindness, what pitiful self-deception!

In order to understand this, we do not by any means have to go as far as the dominant natural-scientific understanding of the world demands: We do not have to view the world as a dead chaos, as a mechanism of lifeless physical and chemical forces. This view, which even today many consider to be the highest achievement of exact scientific knowledge, only attests to the narrowness, soullessness, and scientific obtuseness at which the whole of "progressive" humanity has arrived. The ancient Greeks knew better than we that the world is not a dead machine but a living being, that it is full of living and animate forces. Happily, that spiritual crisis which mankind is living through at the present time has already opened the eyes of many of the most acute of the natural scientists of our time and enabled them to understand the poverty and falseness of the purely mechanical natural-scientific view of the world. Everywhere and on all sides — in the new critique of the mechanical physics of Galileo and Newton, in the new physical theories according to which inert matter is actually composed of bundles of forces, in the critique of the Darwinian theories of evolution, in the discovery of the vitalistic anti-mechanistic principles of organic life — it is again becoming clear to the human gaze that the world is not a dead chaos of inert material particles, but something much more complex and vital. The reproach first addressed by the Russian poet to his contemporaries is now repeated by many representatives of science:

47

They do not see and do not hear,
They live in this world as in darkness.
For them even suns do not breathe
And there is no life in the sea's waves . . .[7]

The world is not a dead machine or a chaos of inert matter: "It is not a soulless mask."[8] Rather, the world is a great living being and, at the same time, the unity of a multitude of living forces.

Nevertheless, the world is not a seeing and rational being. The world is a blind giant, writhing in torment, torn apart by his own passions — a giant gnawing at himself in pain and not finding an outlet to his powers. And inasmuch as man is an element in the world's composition, a tiny part and product of the world, a tiny cell or molecule of the world's body; and inasmuch as his soul is only a particle of this cosmic soul and is subject to the forces of the latter — he is hopelessly enchained, enslaved by the powerful blind forces of the cosmos, and at the same time he is doomed to writhe in meaningless torment, to be meaninglessly born, to rush somewhere, and to perish fruitlessly in the blind process of the unceasing vortex of cosmic life. And we have already seen that the ancient Greeks, enthralled by the beauty and living harmony of the cosmic whole, had a bitter and inconsolably despairing awareness of the hopelessness, vanity, and meaninglessness of human life in this whole.

Wherever we cast our glance, whatever side of life we look at — insofar as we are honestly attempting to gain a knowledge of the empirical essence of life, objectively given to us — we become convinced of the fateful meaninglessness of life. We have seen what the conditions of the attainability of the meaning of life are: first, the existence of God as the absolute Good, as eternal Life and the eternal light of the Truth; and second, the divinity of man, the possibility for man to participate in this true divine life, to ground himself upon it, to wholly fill with it his own life. But the world is not God, and the world's life is not divine life. Pantheism asserts the opposite, but the only thing this assertion can do is abstractly tempt some

7. These lines are from a poem by Fyodor Tyutchev (1803-1873), one of Russia's greatest poets. *Trans.*

8. This line is from the same poem by Tyutchev. *Trans.*

people, whereas in living experience we are too clearly conscious of the fact that the world is not the same thing as God: The world is dominated by death; it is subject to the all-annihilating flux of time; it is full of darkness and blindness. And if the world is such, is it legitimate to deduce the existence of God from the existence of the world? All the attempts of human thought to arrive at the recognition of God *by this path* have turned out to be and turn out to be futile. However enthralled we might be by the harmony and magnificence of the world, by the beauty and complexity of the beings living in it; however great our awe might be before the measurelessness of its depths, both when we contemplate the starry sky and when we are conscious of our own souls — the presence in it of suffering, evil, blindness, and corruption contradict the world's divinity and do not permit us to see in it — as it is and as it is immediately given to us — decisive evidence of the presence of an all-knowing, all-good, and all-powerful Creator. As Max Scheler, an astute contemporary German religious thinker, says, "If we attempt, starting from the knowledge of the world, to deduce the existence of God, the presence in the world of even a single worm writhing in pain would be a decisive counterargument to such a deduction."

In observing the world as it is, we inevitably arrive at a dilemma in the question of its first cause or of the action of God in it. Here are the horns of the dilemma: Either God does not exist at all, and the world was created by a meaningless and blind power; or God, as the all-good and all-knowing being, exists, but in that case He is not omnipotent, not the Creator and the sovereign Providence of the world. The first conclusion is the one drawn by the currently dominant worldview; the second conclusion, more profound, was affirmed by the Gnostics on the basis of purely religious motives, and in the modern period has been drawn by a number of thinkers who are seeking God on a purely intellectual path. But in both cases — both if God does not exist and if He is powerless to help us and to save us from the world's evil and meaninglessness — our life is equally meaningless. But, as we have seen, even God's existence is insufficient to give meaning to our life. What is needed for this is the possibility of our own human participation in the light and life of Divinity. What is needed is the eternity, the perfect enlightenment and peace of our own human life. But this condition (irrespective of its difficulty in all

49

other respects) is absolutely unrealizable insofar as man is a part and product of cosmic nature with all its blindness, imperfection, and corruptibility. In order to believe in the attainability of the meaning of life, we are, as it were, compelled to deny the indisputable fact that man is enslaved by and permeated by the forces of nature — we are compelled to go against the self-evidence of this unalterable fact. Does this not mean that a positive solution to the problem of the meaning of life, that a real acquisition of this meaning, is impossible; and that our fate is to impotently dream of this meaning, while clearly perceiving the absolute unrealizability of our dream?

The meaninglessness of life is not something that was revealed only yesterday. As we have seen, ancient wisdom declared that life was meaningless with perhaps a greater power and clarity than is accessible to contemporary man, who has lost the integral perception of life and therefore has the tendency to become inebriated with illusions. Nevertheless, from time immemorial, mankind has possessed the religious consciousness, has believed in God and in the possibility of the salvation of man, and with this belief has affirmed the realizability of the meaning of life. Is this a mere inconsistency? Has mankind been unable or afraid to draw the final conclusion from indisputable facts? Such a judgment would be a hasty and thoughtless conclusion on our part. On the contrary, we must reflect more deeply on the matter, more fully assess the motives governing mankind's religious consciousness, and ask ourselves the following question: Is a deduction made from the empirical nature of the world and of life the sufficient and unique criterion for solving the problem of the meaning of life?

V

The Self-Evident Character of True Being

Having posed this question, we must immediately answer it in the negative. The fact of the matter is that we just cannot be satisfied with the conclusion that life is totally meaningless. We cannot be satisfied with this conclusion (apart from everything else that is wrong with it) if only because it contains an *internal logical contradiction.* Specifically, it contradicts a simple, self-evident fact (and, because of its self-evident character, a fact that is usually not noticed): the fact that *we understand and rationally affirm this meaninglessness.* The fact that we understand and rationally affirm it means that not everything in the world is meaningless: there at least exists meaningful knowledge, even if this is knowledge only of the meaninglessness of the world's being. The fact that we *clearly see* our blindness means that we are not completely blind, that we can to some extent see. A being absolutely and wholly devoid of meaning could not be conscious of its own meaninglessness. If the world and life were a total chaos of blind, meaningless forces, there could not exist in them a being who would be conscious of this and could express it. Just as the assertion "truth does not exist" is meaningless because it is contradictory (since the one who asserts this considers his assertion to be true and thus at the same time both recognizes and rejects the existence of truth), so the assertion that life is totally and universally meaningless is itself meaningless, since, being an act of rational knowledge, it, in itself, represents a fact that refutes its content.

The response to this will of course be that this traditional objection is an empty and pitiful sophism, based on a play of words. In asserting the meaninglessness of life, we have in mind (as we ourselves clarified above) the absence in life of the absolute good and of the possibility of filling our lives with this good; that is, in asserting the meaninglessness of life, we deny the existence of God and the divinity of man. The fact that we can perceive and understand this "absence" does not change anything in its content. In other words, the fact that the assertion of the meaninglessness of life is itself rational and, in *this* sense, "meaningful" knowledge does not in the slightest shake the content of this assertion, for here "meaning" signifies nothing more than theoretical groundedness or self-evidence, and by no means that practical life-meaning which we are seeking. On the contrary, the existence of the *consciousness* of the meaninglessness of life does not diminish this meaninglessness but increases it; because of its impotence and purposelessness, this very consciousness attests to the profound meaninglessness of life: Why, in this blind chaos, should the existence of human thought be necessary if it cannot help anything, if it cannot save us from the meaninglessness of life, but only condemns us to impotent suffering from it? Is this not, on the contrary, a particularly meaningless mockery of man by cosmic fate — this imparting to him of spiritual sight so that he could see his impotence before the blind forces of the universe and be tormented by them without any recourse?

This argument has a certain amount of truth, which consists in the fact that reason, in the sense of a simple capacity for theoretical knowledge, cannot of course save us and replace for us the sought-for integral meaning of life. But let us not be hasty; let us not too rapidly skirt this fact of the existence in us of reason and content ourselves with a superficial assessment of this fact. However insufficient reason might be in itself, it is nevertheless a slit of light at which we must look attentively.

Thus, the world is organized in such a way that, even though it is blind and meaningless in its course, in its active forces, nevertheless in the element of human reason it is permeated by a beam of light, illuminated by *knowledge of itself*. This light of knowledge — however insufficient it might be for the purpose of transfiguring the world and dissipating its darkness, since it can only see this darkness, not overcome it — is nevertheless something absolutely heterogeneous in relation to this darkness and in general to all the forces and realities of the empirical world. Knowledge is neither a physical collision of realities nor some kind of interaction between them. It is a wholly original principle, indescribable in terms of empirical reality, a principle by virtue of which being is revealed or illuminated, is conscious of itself and knows itself. Despite its real impotence, this principle, in its originality and incomparability, is a great and miraculous fact. Inquiring into this principle, Pascal called man a "thinking reed" and said that "if the entire universe were to collapse on top of me and crush me, at this instant of my death I would nevertheless surpass the universe, for it would not know what it was doing, but *I would know it*."[1] Man is an insignificant reed shaken by every gust of wind, a weak sprout perishing from the slightest action of the hostile cosmic forces; but by his rational consciousness he rises above the entire world, for he surveys it. Born for a brief instant, powerlessly carried along by the rapid flow of time and condemned by the latter to inevitable death, man possesses eternity in his consciousness and knowledge, for his gaze can hover over both the infinite past and the infinite future; it can know the eternal truths and the eternal foundation of life. We will be told that it is a poor consolation to be conscious that one is perishing. Yes, it is a poor consolation, but it is nevertheless a consolation or the possible beginning of consolation. For, at least in our knowledge, we already clearly do not belong to this world and are not subject to its meaningless forces; we touch something beyond the world; we find a small point of support there, which is nevertheless a genuine support, fixed and unshakable.

Our knowledge, which is clearly supraspatial and supratemporal (for it is capable of surveying and knowing both infinite space and infinite time), represents in us the principle of another, eternal being, the action in us of a certain supramundane, divine power (although this action is obscured by our sensuous limitedness and weakness). In knowledge there is revealed for us a completely special, supra-empirical and, at the same time, absolutely evident being — most proximately, the inner being of us ourselves. This self-evident inner being in all its contradistinction from all that is external and empirically given to us was first

---

1. The italics in this quotation are Frank's. *Trans.*

recognized and described by St. Augustine. With regard to *this* being, Augustine says,

> We are not disturbed by any possible confusion of truth with false-hood, for we do not come into contact with it by some bodily sense, the way we come into contact with the things outside of us. . . . But without any delusive representation of images or phantasms, I am absolutely certain that I am. . . . For if I am deceived, I am. For he who does not exist, cannot be deceived. . . . And since I am if I am deceived, how am I deceived in believing that I am, for it is certain that I am if I am deceived? Since, therefore, I, the person deceived, should be, even if I were deceived, certainly I am not deceived in this knowledge that I am.[2]

And together with this inner being of us ourselves, a being which is so distinctive and so supra-empirical, there is immediately revealed to us something much more significant — the self-evident and self-grounded being of the Truth itself, although here it is revealed only in the one-sided form of the light of theoretical knowledge. For in the act of our knowledge it is not we ourselves who do something; and it is not out of us ourselves, as limited and separate beings, that something is born. All we do is recognize the truth; we are illuminated by the light of knowledge, the self-evidence of that which truly is, irrespective of whether we know it or not, of whether it is revealed to our consciousness or not. Therefore, despite all its self-evidence, our own being is not the first and self-sufficient self-evidence; our own being would not be revealed to us and we would not have knowledge of it if, in being itself as such, the principle of Knowledge were not present, the primordial light of the Truth, which in all human knowledge illuminates the human soul. This light of the Truth, one for all (for truth is one for all), is eternal, for truth itself does not change from the present day to tomorrow, but is valid once and for always; and this light is also all-embracing, for there is nothing that is fundamentally inaccessible to illumination by knowledge, however weak and limited

---

2. From *The City of God*, XI, 26. Here I have made use, in a slightly modified form, of the Marcus Dods translation (reprint, New York: The Modern Library, 1950, p. 370). *Trans.*

might be the human knowledge of each of us. This light of the Truth is clearly not something that is merely human; nor is it something that is only from the world; nor is it something particular and conditioned in general. Without exhausting the inexpressible fullness and vitality of Divinity, this light is a reflection and revelation of Divinity in our own consciousness and being. And it is for this reason that, together with our own being and its self-consciousness, there is revealed to us, as its condition, the self-evident and self-grounded being of the Truth itself and our groundedness upon it. This too was clearly recognized and expressed by St. Augustine: "Everyone who recognizes that he doubts is conscious of something true and is certain of what he recognizes; that is, he is certain of something true. Thus, anyone who doubts the existence of truth has in himself something true which he does not doubt, and something that is true cannot be such except in virtue of the Truth" (*De vera religione*, c. 39).[3] Also: "I asked myself: 'Is Truth then nothing at all, simply because it has no extension in space, with or without limits?' And, far off, I heard your voice saying, *I am the God who IS*. I heard your voice, as we hear voices that speak to our hearts, and at once I had no cause to doubt. I might more easily have doubted that I was alive than that Truth had being."[4]

Thus, the simple and imperceptible fact of our knowledge — even if this is only knowledge of the meaninglessness and darkness of our life — assures us not only of the certainty of our own, inner supra-empirical being, but also of the certainty of the eternal, all-embracing Divine being, of the supramundane principle of Truth, if only as the light of pure knowledge. Inquiring into the fact of knowledge and its nature, we discover for the first time, alongside the empirical objective world, the presence of *absolute* being (if only in its indistinct and most general contours) and the fact that we directly and primordially belong to this being. And this opens new horizons in the question of the meaning of life. However painful for us the meaninglessness of all of empirical life might be, whatever difficulties this meaninglessness might cause for us in the search for the

---

3. This is translated from Frank's Russian version. *Trans.*
4. *The Confessions*, VII, 10. I have used R. S. Pine-Coffin's translation (New York: Penguin Books, 1961, p. 147). *Trans.*

meaning of life, we now begin to understand for the first time that we have sought this meaning where there is no hope of finding it, and that being is scarcely exhausted by this dark and chaotic domain. We have not yet explored that primordial, deeper stratum of being which is given to us in our own inner being, which is immediately revealed in us, and in those ultimate, absolute depths which we touch in our inner being. Our horizons have expanded; an entire new world of true, spiritual being (a world that is immeasurably more profound, significant, and stable than the other one) has become visible for the first time, if only dimly and partially. It belongs to the very essence of empirical life as such (whether it be our personal life or cosmic life) that this life is meaningless, that it cannot satisfy the conditions under which the meaning of life can be realized. This meaninglessness belongs to the very essence of empirical life and derives, if from nothing else, from the fact that this life is subject to the flux of time, that it, to use Plato's words, "only arises and perishes, but does not have being." And the true wisdom of all times and nations has known this. But empirical life does not by any means exhaust true being; and it is at the latter that we must now direct our spiritual gaze.

We are guided to true being not only by the fact of knowledge which has been illuminated with meaning. After all, it is not the case that we only have dispassionately objective knowledge of the fact of the meaninglessness of life. We are also anguished by this knowledge, are dissatisfied with it, and seek the meaning of life. Even if our seekings turn out to be futile, they represent a highly significant fact which belongs to the reality of our inner being. Let us cast our gaze upon ourselves and ask, Where does our anguish come from? Where does this dissatisfaction come from, this fact of our being drawn to something fundamentally different, to something that, as we have seen, so sharply and decisively contradicts all the empirical data of life? If earlier we had observed that a being wholly submerged in and embraced by the cosmic meaninglessness could not *know* this meaninglessness, then now we are right to add that such a being could not suffer from this meaninglessness, could not be outraged at it and seek the meaning of life. If human beings were truly only blind animals, moved only by the elemental passions of self-preservation and the preservation of the genus, they, like all other animals, would not be anguished by the meaninglessness of life and would not seek its meaning. The striving for the absolute good, eternal life, and the fullness of satisfaction that lies at the basis of this anguish and seeking; this thirst to find God, to commune with Him, and to find peace in Him — this too is *a great fact of the reality* of man's being. And a more attentive examination of human life readily discloses that this entire life — despite all the blindness, viciousness, and darkness of its empirical forces — is an obscure and distorted manifestation of this fundamental fact. When we seek riches, pleasures, or honor; when — in a cowardly manner in relation to ourselves and coldly and cruelly in relation to our neighbors — we struggle for our own existence; and especially when we seek forgetfulness and consolation in love or practical activity — in all these cases we *essentially* seek one thing: to "save" ourselves, to find the genuine ground for our being and genuinely nourishing food for our spirit. We always seek — if blindly and in a distorted manner — the absolute good and true life. Where does all this come from? And why is it that our souls cannot be satisfied with the limits and possibilities of empirical life but, even if only secretly and semiconsciously, seek the impossible? Whence comes this disharmony between the human soul and *the entire world* into whose composition the soul itself enters?

> Whence comes this disharmony?
> And why is it that in the common choir
> The soul does not sing the same song as the sea?
> And why does the thinking reed complain?[5]

True, the adherents of the naturalistic and positivistic worldview will offer the following objection: However difficult it might be to answer the question "Whence?" this question cannot in any case take us beyond the limits of this world and guide us to a path leading to the discovery of the meaning of life. For, given the blindness of the forces acting in the world, there is nothing surprising in the fact that not everything in the world is ordered harmoniously and that, in particular, we, human beings, are endowed with the sad trait of aspiring to the impossible and fruitlessly suffering. Just as a moth blindly flies toward a

---

5. These lines are from a poem by Tyutchev. *Trans.*

flame and perishes in it, so we just as blindly pass by, without satisfaction, real empirically given life-possibilities and ruin ourselves, even often ending in suicide, in the search for what does not exist on earth, in meaningless and objectless anguish. Consequently, this anguish, implanted in our hearts from birth, is yet one more datum of evidence that life is meaningless and blindly elemental.

Nevertheless, as soon as we subject to careful scrutiny this fact of our inner life and feel it in all its immeasurable significance, there involuntarily arises in us a wholly different way of looking at things: Not this fact, but precisely the entire world that is in disharmony with it, appears to us then to be a strange misunderstanding. It is not we who must correct ourselves and, for the sake of sober adaptation to the empirical possibilities, forget about this primordial ground of our being; rather, the entire world must become different, in order to give room and satisfaction to this inalienable aspiration of ours, to this most profound essence of our "I." It begins to dimly appear to us that the fact that a two-legged animal called man is not able to calmly establish himself on earth and that an incomprehensible inner dissatisfaction fills him with anguish (a fact which is so insignificant and trivial from the point of view of the objective empirical world), this fact is — for the gaze directed inward and into the depths — evidence that we belong to a wholly other, deeper, fuller, and more rational being. Let it be the case that we are powerless prisoners of this world and that our revolt, by virtue of its powerlessness, is a meaningless undertaking. Nevertheless, we are only the prisoners, not the citizens, of this world: We have a dim memory of our true homeland, and do not envy those who could forget completely about it; toward them we experience only contempt or compassion, despite all their worldly successes and all our suffering. And if this true spiritual homeland of ours, this primordial soil for our spiritual nourishment, for the possibility of true life, is precisely what people call God, then we understand the profound meaning of St. Augustine's words: "Thou madest us for Thyself, and our heart is restless until it repose in Thee."[6]

There is one consideration which helps us to justify this dim consciousness and to refute the complacently pitiful explanation of natural-

6. *The Confessions*, I, 1. This is taken from the Pusey translation. *Trans.*

ism. Let it be the case that we do not know the source of this anguished longing in us for true life and the absolute good, and that we are doubtful as to its significance. But let us inquire into the very content of *that toward which we are aspiring,* and pose this question: Where does this content come from, and what does it signify? And then at once, if we attentively inquire into the matter, we will learn that all the possibilities of the naturalistic explanation come to an end here. For *precisely because* there is nothing in the empirical world that corresponds to the object of our aspirations, it becomes impossible to explain how this world could have gained dominion over our consciousness and what in general it signifies. We seek the absolute good, but in the world all goods are relative, all are only means to something else. In the final analysis, they are means to the preservation of our life, which in itself is by no means an indisputable and absolute good. Where does our *concept* of the absolute good come from? We seek eternal life, for all temporal things are meaningless; but, in the world, all things — including us ourselves — are temporal. But where then does our *concept* of the eternal come from? We seek the peace and self-groundedness of life-fullness — but in the world and in our life we know only agitation, the transition from one thing to another, partial satisfaction, accompanied by need or by the boredom of satiety. Where does this concept of the blissful peace of satisfaction come from?

Some might retort, "Any number of things can provoke insane dreams in the sick human brain!" But those who give such a facile answer to this question do not have any idea of its difficulty. We are inquiring here not into the origin of the fact of our dreams, but into the *content* of the object of this fact. All other human dreams, even the most insane and unrealizable ones, have as their object some empirical content of life, known from experience: When we dream — without any foundation — that we will suddenly inherit a great fortune, or that we will become famous, or that we will win the love of the most beautiful woman in the world, our dreams are always rooted in things that happen in the world, even if only rarely, and that are familiar to us, if only by rumor, from the experience of this world. Or, in the worst case, our dream quantitatively exaggerates the reality given in experience; but here we are striving to attain something that, even on a quantitatively small scale, we have never encountered and never seen in the world, even something that we *could never have* seen and known, because — by its very concept, by its qualitative content — it is not possible for it to exist in the world. Consequently, the object of our dream has a supramundane, supra-empirical content: it is something *other than the whole world,* and at the same time it is *given to us.* This is a fact upon which one cannot fail to reflect; it reveals to us broad yet unexplored horizons. Are we not in fact *given* precisely that which we seek? Are we not already in possession of that which is sought?

I foresee that the reader, indignant or puzzled, will once again object that this is merely a pitiful sophism! The object of our dreams is given, but, after all, it is given precisely only as the object of our *dreams.* It is given to us as a good imagined by us, and not at all in reality. It is given in the same way that your thought is "given" an object which you seek, in the same way that a lost treasure is "given" which has been buried somewhere. It is not given as a good which one possesses and can enjoy. Must we be satisfied with an "imagined" God, with an imagined "truth of life"?

Psychologically, this objection is totally natural. It also has a deeper objective meaning, which we will attempt to clarify below. But in general, in the immediate sense in which it is expressed, this objection is based on an inattentive consideration of the spiritual problem and on a false enslavement by a one-sided, purely sensuously empirical concept of reality.

The Gospel says, "Seek, and ye shall find; knock, and it shall be opened unto you" (Matt. 7:7; Luke 11:9). A genuine understanding of the profound divine truth contained in these words is by no means based on some "blind," unexamined faith in authority; rather, such an understanding is given to that faith which is a directedness of the gaze at spiritual being and a perception of the nature of the latter. One who has directed his gaze at spiritual being knows that the meaning and truth of these words consist in the fact that, in spiritual being, all seeking is already a partial possession, and every knock on the closed door is already an opening of it.

In the empirical world, that which is "imagined" and merely "sought" differs essentially from that which is "real" and "present," for here "reality" means for us the presence of an object for our sensuous gaze, its sensuous proximity to us, its accessibility to our active will. In this sense there is (as Kant pointed out in his critique of the so-called ontological proof of the existence of God) a colossal, totally insuperable practical difference between "one hundred thalers in my pocket" and "one hundred imagined thalers," even though there is a complete identity of the objects that are thought; the first "one hundred thalers" give us satisfaction, are useful to us in a practical way, whereas the second "one hundred thalers" only lure us with an illusory dream, but "in reality" (that is, for our pockets, for the filling of our hungry stomachs) are absent, do not exist. Here, "to exist" means to be somewhere, some time, in someone's possession; it means to be visible and tangible, to be in sensuous proximity, within the horizon of the subject of knowledge. And an object can be thought and can be an object of dream and imagination without existing here and now, without being present. But, in the spiritual world and in relation to objects of a spiritual order, can we consider possible and satisfactory *such* a concept of existence and the correlative concept of simple "imaginability"?

It is obvious that, in this case, "to exist" cannot mean to be present here, in front of me, in sensuous proximity to me, to be visible, audible, tangible; for objects of the spiritual order — such as bliss, eternity, or reason — cannot in general "exist" in *such* a manner. "To exist" here simply means to be self-evident, to be clearly present before the spiritual gaze, before one's mental vision. But once we seek these objects of a spiritual order, and in our seeking "think" or "imagine" them, that is, have them mentally before ourselves; and once we have become convinced that they are not a product of our subjective fantasy, combining or exaggerating material of the sensuous world, but are rather certain *primary* contents — these objects then *exist* for us, even if in the most obscure form. To ask whether they "really" exist is just as meaningless as to ask whether a number or a mathematical concept thought by me "really" exists. One can rationally ask whether I can possess this object, commune with it, merge with it. But one cannot ask whether it itself exists.

Anyone who has intensely thought about what the nature is of the true goodness, bliss, or eternity which he seeks, that person *thus* knows that *something like this exists.* Let it be the case that this something contradicts all the possibilities of the empirical world and that we have never encountered it in our sensuous experience; let it be the case that it is paradoxical and improbable from the point of view of common human experience and all our well-worn notions and dominant interests — but if our heart draws us to it and our gaze is therefore directed at it, we *see* it, and therefore it *exists*. I can think that this something is not realizable in the empirical world, that it is powerless in the face of the blind forces of life, which have driven it to distant regions beyond the bounds of the world, regions in which it is accessible only to my seeking soul — but there, powerless and remote from the entire world, it nevertheless *exists*, and nothing prevents me from loving it and being drawn to it. Moreover, I involuntarily notice, even if rarely, the presence — or at least the faint manifestation or reflection — of this something in my life: The sincere greeting, the soulful caress of another person, his kind gaze directed at me — this tells me that goodness lives and is manifested in him, even if only remotely. Every act of self-renunciation shows me that animal passions and cold, calculating greed are not the only forces that operate in life; and at rare times, at completely exceptional moments of my life, I am capable not only of dreaming of eternity or of the fullness of satisfaction but also of *experiencing them* for a brief instant, of feeling that they have been realized. What I am seeking not only exists; its rays reach the world and act upon the world.

And if I turn now to my own personal *search* for the meaning of life, I clearly see that this search — despite its apparent unrealizability — *is itself a manifestation in me of the reality of that which I seek*. The search for God is already an action of God in the human soul. Not only does God exist in general (otherwise we would not be able to think Him and seek Him, so dissimilar is that which we seek here to all that is familiar to us from sensuous experience), but *He is also precisely with us or within us*. He acts within us, and precisely His action is manifested in our strange agitation and dissatisfaction, so purposeless and incomprehensible from the point of view of the world — in our search for what does not exist in the world: "Thou madest us for Thyself, and our heart is restless until it repose in Thee."

Goodness, eternity, the fullness of blissful satisfaction, the light of truth — all these things which we need if our life is to acquire "meaning" — are not an empty dream, not an invention of human imagination. Rather, they *really exist*, which is attested to by our own existence, by our thought about this, by our own search for it. We resemble those near-sighted and absentminded people who search for their lost glasses and cannot find them because their glasses are perched on their nose, and the seekers *are looking through* them as they search. The same St. Augustine said, "Go not abroad but enter into yourself: truth dwells in the inner man; and if you should find your nature mutable, transcend yourself."[7] If we unlearn the habit of considering that the sole reality is that which surrounds us from outside, that which we see and touch, and that which pushes us, torments us, and whirls us about in an obscure eddy; and if we direct our attention to the great reality of our own being, of our inner world — we will become convinced that, in the world, *not everything* is meaningless and blind, that in the world — in our own anguish and seeking, and in that light which we seek and thus dimly see — there operate forces and principles of another order, precisely those which we seek. To be sure, there are many people who appear to be abandoned by God, who in their entire life will not have an inkling of this — just as an infant cannot direct his mental gaze at himself and, crying and rejoicing, know what is happening with him, or see his own reality. But the fact that man is blind and slow-witted, the fact that he wears blinders which permit him to look ahead but do not let him look around him — this does not refute the reality of that which his gaze does not see. This reality is with us and within us; every sigh of our anguish, every impulse of our deepest essence, is an action of this reality and, therefore, evidence of it. All we have to do is learn, as Plato said, "to turn the eyes of the soul" in order to see that by which "we live, and move, and have our being" (Acts 17:28).

And now we can combine these two conditions of the meaning of life which we have found. An analysis of our understanding of the "meaninglessness" of life has shown us that, in this understanding, the action of existent Truth is manifested as the light of knowledge. Further, we have seen that, in our very seeking, in our dissatisfaction with the meaninglessness of life, there are revealed the presence and action of principles which are *opposite* to this meaninglessness. These two elements are not as unconnected as it might have seemed at the very beginning. For in the

---

7. *On True Religion*, 39, 72. *Trans.*

very *knowledge* of the meaninglessness of life, in the cold theoretical observation of this meaninglessness, there is, of course, unconsciously contained an element of the search for meaning, an element of dissatisfaction. Otherwise, we would not be able to form a theoretical judgment presupposing an *evaluation* of life from the point of view of its sought ideal. And, on the other hand, we would not be able to search for anything or consciously yearn for anything if, in general, we were not conscious beings, if we were not able to *know* our need and what we need to satisfy it. However frequently the cold judgment of our thought might diverge on the surface of our consciousness from the unuttered and uncomprehended impulse of our being, in the ultimate depths these two elements are fused in an indissoluble unity. We desire to *know* in order to live; but to live means, on the other hand, to live not in blindness and darkness, but in the light of knowledge. We seek living knowledge and knowing life, life illuminated with knowledge. The light not only illuminates; it also warms; and the power of its burning heats us to an intense incandescent radiance. True life, which we seek and the obscure beating of which we feel in ourselves in this very seeking, is the unity of life and truth. It is life that is not only illuminated by light, but that is also fused with light. It is "illuminated life." And in the ultimate depths of our being we feel that the light of knowledge and the supreme good of life that we seek are two aspects of one and the same principle. We are conscious of that which is supra-empirical and absolute in us as both the light of knowledge and the eternal good — as that inexpressible supreme principle which the Russian language designates by the untranslatable and inexhaustible word *pravda*.[8]

And precisely this absolute, this living reason or rational life, this existent, illuminating, and warming *pravda* (truth as righteousness), self-evidently *is*. It is *true being*, immediately given to us or, rather, revealed in us. It is more certain than everything else on earth, for about everything that is given to us from outside, one can ask, Does it exist or not? But about true being, one cannot ask whether it exists, for this *very question*

---

8. One way to translate this "untranslatable" word is "truth as justice or righteousness." Words derived from *pravda* include *opravdanie* (justification) and *pravdivyi* (righteous). *Trans.*

is already a revelation of true being, and an affirmative answer here *precedes the very question,* as the condition of its possibility. Somewhere in the depths of our own being, far from everything which is possible in the world and by which the world lives, and which is also closer than everything else, *in us ourselves* or on that threshold which unites the ultimate depths of our "I" with the still greater, ultimate depths of being — somewhere in these depths there is *Pravda,* true and absolute being. And this being pulsates in us and demands an outlet for itself, demands to be manifested — it desires to inundate with the beams of its light and warm our entire life and the life of the entire world; and precisely this pulsation of this being, this immediate manifestation of it, is that insatiable and anguished yearning for the meaning of life which torments us. We are no longer alone in our seekings, and our seekings do not appear to us to be as hopeless as before.

• VI •

The Justification of Faith

But, of course, this too is not enough. As we know, what we need if we want to find the truly essential meaning of life is, first of all, the existence of God as the absolute foundation for the forces of goodness, reason, and eternity, the foundation which guarantees that these forces will triumph over the forces of evil, meaninglessness, and corruption; and second, the possibility that I personally, in my weak and brief life, can commune with God and fill my life with Him. But to realize both of these desires simultaneously appears to be absolutely impossible, for they seem to contradict each other.

God is the unity of all-goodness with all-powerfulness. We believe in God insofar as we believe that the good is not only an existent principle, a genuine supramundane reality, but also the *unique* true reality, which therefore possesses absolute all-powerfulness. A powerless god is not God; and in a previous discussion we were too hasty in giving the name "God" to the existent good we found. Does not the meaninglessness of life which torments us consist precisely in the fact that the rays of light and goodness in life are so faint that they only dimly and from afar penetrate the thick surrounding layer of darkness and evil, that they are barely visible to us, and that life is dominated by principles opposite to light and goodness? Let it be the case that Truth[1] genuinely exists in be-

---

1. Here and in the further discussion in this chapter, the Russian word that is translated as "Truth" is *Pravda,* meaning "truth as justice or righteousness." *Trans.*

ing; but Truth is lost and powerless in being. It is enslaved by hostile powers and is defeated by them at every step; the world's life remains meaningless.

And so, especially, does our personal life. We, or in any case each one of us, are enslaved by cosmic forces of evil and blindness; eddies of these forces grasp us outwardly and confound us inwardly; our life is broken apart and carried away by the flow of time; and *within us* we lack in any case the self-grounded peace, the luminous clarity, the fullness of being, that we need to make our life meaningful. And only dimly and with great difficulty do we come to understand that we are in contact with another principle — with Truth; and this Truth lives in us as a faint, powerless spark, barely glimmering in the fog of life (as *Fünklein,* which is what Meister Eckhart called the divine principle within us). But we need this Truth to fill our entire life, to dissolve our entire life in itself.

Both conditions turn out to be unrealized. Furthermore, we appear to clearly see that they are unrealizable. For if, despite the meaningless-ness of all of empirical life, we can recognize the very existence of the Truth as a special supramundane and supra-empirical principle, never-theless we evidently do not have the right to recognize the all-powerfulness or all-unity of the Truth, outside us and within us, for its all-powerfulness and all-unity would contradict the indisputable fact of the meaninglessness of life.

There are no logical tricks, no subtle arguments, that can resolve this contradiction, that can honestly, completely, and convincingly overcome it. Nevertheless, our heart overcomes it; and in faith, in the special, su-preme act of "knowledge of the heart," we clearly perceive the self-evident presence of the conditions for the meaning of life — the self-evidence of the all-powerfulness of the Truth and the total and perfect groundedness of us ourselves, of our entire being, in the Truth. And this faith is not just a "blind" faith, not *credo quia absurdum,* but with logical paradoxicality, with "improbability," it combines a higher, perfect cer-tainty and self-evidence. And it is only because of our weakness that, in life, we constantly lose the previously gained self-evidence and, tor-mented by doubt, begin once again to think that this self-evidence is "improbable."

When with the greatest intensity of our spiritual will we enter with our thought or, rather, with our life and feeling into that supreme principle which is clearly present before us as the existent Truth — it becomes perfectly evident to us that this Truth and genuine Being *are one and the same thing*. The Truth not only is; and it is not only the *Truth*. It is also that which, in the ultimate and most profound sense, we call *life* or *being;* it is our absolutely firm and unique *soil;* and without it, all things hang in the air and come to a standstill. The Truth is that the opposite of which is non-being, death, disappearance. In it, all things are strengthened, acquire stability and fullness, blossom and breathe fully. Without it, all things dry up, pale, fade, and perish. And although, in a de facto sense, many things exist besides the Truth — the entire empirical world with its multitude of entities — nevertheless, insofar as we conceive this world as really existing outside the absolute Truth, it becomes a shadow, a phantom, the darkness of non-being, and we stop understanding how it could exist. Whatever our everyday experience might tell us, there lives in the depths of our being a higher criterion of truth, which clearly perceives that there is nothing outside of God and that we "live, and move, and have our being" only in Him.

We can approach this self-evident — although mysterious — truth from different directions. Here we will mention those directions which, although suprarational, lend themselves most readily to rational expression.

We have seen that the composition of the existent Truth includes an element according to which this Truth is the light of knowledge, theoretical truth or contemplation, the revelation of being. But, in the genuine and ultimate sense, to be means to be conscious or to know. Totally unconscious being is not being; to be means to be *for oneself,* to be revealed to oneself, to be a self-consciousness. It is true that we see around ourselves a multitude of things and entities which we call unconscious, inanimate, and even dead; and we know that our bodies are fated to become such "dead" things, and with a shudder of horror we are conscious that this is actually the case. All of these dead, inanimate entities and things *exist;* they exist precisely "for us," because we know them or are conscious of them, but they do not exist for themselves. But although this is the case, we do not really understand how this is possible, and precisely this fact is the greatest problem of philosophy. And, grounding ourselves on our personal experience, on the concept of being which we derive from our personal being (and in the final analysis, where else could we get our concept of being?), we arrive at the conviction that *either* these dead things do not exist at all *in themselves,* but "exist" *only* "for us," that is, as representations of our consciousness, and thus do not exist in the true sense; *or* that (and this is the final conclusion, owing to the unsatisfactoriness of the first thesis), existing in themselves, these things — if only in an embryonic, obscure, potential form — exist *for themselves* as well, are conscious of themselves, are fading, barely smoldering sparks of the absolute Light. That which exists *lives* in some manner (even if only embryonically); and that which *lives* is animate and conscious in some manner (again, even if only embryonically). In the ultimate depths of being, there is nothing except light; and it is only on the surface of being that we see — either because of the distortion of being itself or because our vision is poor — blindness and darkness. But absolute darkness is just as meaningless as absolute non-being: There is no non-being; everything that is is being; and therefore everything that is is being for itself, the light of knowledge, a revelation of existent truth. And we understand that the light is not a random principle which has come into the world from somewhere and gotten lost in it, and which is at risk of being extinguished at any moment, of being destroyed by the darkness. We recognize, on the contrary, that the light is the beginning and essence of all things, that light and being are one and the same — the unique truly Existent: "In the beginning was the Word, and the Word was with God, and the Word was God. The same was in the beginning with God. All things were made by him; and without him was not any thing made that was made. In him was life; and the life was the light of men. And the light shineth in darkness; and the darkness comprehended it not" (John 1:1-5).[2]

This supramundane and world-embracing Light is also an eternal principle and, more than that, it is eternity itself. In every truth, even that which is the most empirical in its content and accessible to the

---

2. Frank explores this idea in his book *The Light Shineth in Darkness: An Essay in Christian Ethics and Social Philosophy* (first published in Russian in 1949; English translation by Boris Jakim, Ohio University Press, 1989). *Trans.*

most limited mind, we perceive eternity and look at the world from eternity. For every truth, as such, is a perception of eternal meaning and fixes even a singular and momentary phenomenon forever; every truth is valid once and for always. And insofar as we are conscious of the Light as the primordial ground of being and as the unique genuine being, we know that we are rooted in eternity, that eternity embraces us from all sides, and that the very flux of time is inconceivable except in the bosom of eternity and, as Plato said, in the capacity of "the moving form of eternity." And not only are we clearly conscious of the fact that eternity *exists* (how can that not exist the meaning of which is existence once and for always, the all-embracing and self-grounded fullness and integrality of being?), but we are conscious of the fact that eternity and existence are, strictly speaking, one and the same thing. For that which is not eternal, that which appears and disappears, only passes from non-existence to existence and vice versa, from existence to non-existence. That which is not eternal is first included in and then excluded from existence; and since, in their changeability, all temporal things, in essence, partially perish and are renewed every moment, they *do not exist* at all, but only slide along the threshold of existence, as it were.

And we ourselves, as temporal beings, only slide along the surface of existence; but conscious of all things and of ourselves as well in the light of eternity (there can be no other consciousness of things), at the same time we genuinely *exist* in this consciousness. And insofar as we participate in the eternal light not only with our thought, but also attempt to livingly absorb this light into ourselves, or rather to livingly perceive our primordial rootedness in the eternal light — we know that this genuine or (which is the same thing) eternal being is the ground and ultimate essence of our entire being. Whatever the origin might be of non-eternal, temporal existence, of this all-destroying and all-devouring flux of changeability and corruptibility — we clearly see that this existence is not the essence of being, that it is not a positive and independent force, but only the diminution, unfullness, defectiveness of being. And we clearly see that this defective being is not capable of absorbing eternity, but rather that it itself is possible only on the foundation of eternity. Being and eternity (or eternal life) are *one and the same thing*. Eternity is nothing other than the integral, all-embracing, immediately given full-

70

ness of being; and this eternity is our original possession; it is always ready, as it were, to receive us into its bosom; and it depends only on us, on our spiritual energy and our readiness to make a deep journey into ourselves, whether we go to meet it, or whether we flee from it to that diminished periphery, to that "outer darkness," in which all things are in flux and nothing is stable.

We have seen, further, that the Truth is the supreme good, that it is perfection and the fullness of satisfaction, and that this good, since we perceive it (without which the very search for it would be impossible), necessarily *exists.* But it does not merely "exist," among many other things. Precisely here, that full, adequate knowledge which we have called the "knowledge of the heart," or faith, clearly tells us that the supreme good or perfection is the same thing as being. This knowledge tells us that, really and in the ultimate depths, this supreme good is the only thing that *truly exists;* and it is this good that we have in mind when we speak of being, of that true being which we need and which we seek. For abstract or theoretical knowledge, this is the most difficult and paradoxical affirmation. Do we not see that much that exists in the world, or rather even everything in the world, is imperfect and bad? Do we not even see that, on the contrary, perfection is not realizable in the world and is *only* an object of our dreams, of our impotent yearning? Thus, for cold theoretical knowledge, reality becomes synonymous with imperfection, and perfection becomes synonymous with irreality, only an "ideal," something only imagined, dreamt, immaterial, illusory. And, of course, if we take being to mean empirical existence, the reality of cosmic nature, then that is what it in fact is most proximately and immediately. But it has already been revealed to us that empirical existence, as such, not only does not exhaust being, but does not belong to it at all, is not true being. And at the same time it has been revealed to us that this true being *exists* self-evidently. And when, with our whole essence, we gaze into this true being and consciously experience it, we know that it is precisely what we call perfection or the supreme good.

Here we must recall what we said when we examined the conditions of the possibility of the meaning of life. Mere existence as duration in time and also as the meaningless expenditure of the powers of life in the chase after the preservation of the latter — such existence is, of course, not the supreme good, not the absolute value, but is something that acquires meaning only when it is made to serve the true good. But on the other hand, this true good, which we seek, is not some value with a special, limited content — whether it be pleasure, power, or even the moral good. For all such limited values require justification; in relation to them, the same unavoidable question arises: "For what purpose?" We seek a good which would give fullness of immediate satisfaction and about which no one could ask, "What is its purpose?" And it is precisely this good which we call perfection.

But what does "fullness of immediate satisfaction" mean? What does it mean, in general, to find real, ultimate satisfaction? We have already seen above that it means to find *true life*, the revelation and realization of life, not as poor content, not as a fragment, brief, in flux, and therefore meaningless — but as the all-embracing fullness of being. We seek to attain full, stable, immeasurably rich life, or, simply speaking, we seek to attain life itself in contrast to its illusory and deceptive simulacrum. That consciousness which, in an obscure, distorted form and with false and deceptive content, lives in all of our impulses, passions, and dreams and forms their ultimate and most profound motive force — the consciousness: "We desire *to live*, to live genuinely, and not only to be satisfied with an empty simulacrum of life or with a fruitless waste of life's powers" — this consciousness is the essence of the search for the meaning of life, and expresses our fundamental and primary aspiration. In this sense (as we have seen in Chapter III), it is correct to say that "life is given to us for the sake of life." There is no good greater than life itself — but what is meant here is *genuine life*, as the realization and thorough living-out of the absolute depths of our being, as the creative disclosure of these depths. Life is the same thing as perfection; and since life is nothing else but the inner essence of being as genuine being for itself, as the thorough self-living-out and self-disclosure of being — *being, then, is the same thing as perfection.*

Perfection cannot be only an "ideal." It is not present in anything that does not exist but only "should be." What sort of perfection is it to be only a phantom, a shadow, a dream of the human soul? On the contrary, that which we mean by perfection, that which we seek as the unique absolute good, is *being* itself. The ultimate, absolute depths of being which we yearn for, the ultimate ground of being — *this is the same thing* as the supreme good, perfection, perfect joy, bliss, and luminous peace. This cannot be clarified any further; it cannot be proved in any derivative manner. For the empirical consciousness this is always a paradox or an unsubstantiated assertion, whereas, for the knowledge of the heart, it is a self-evident truth which does not require any proof and which does not admit proof precisely because of its self-evident character. This is a simple description of that by which our heart lives, of that which for the heart is not a subjective "feeling" or "dream," but the self-evidently revealed ultimate depth of that which exists. Ultimate, absolute being is bliss and perfection; and conversely, bliss and perfection are the ultimate, deepest being, the ground of all that exists. This is how the ultimate mystery of being is self-evidently revealed to us. The best example and symbol of this mystery is *love*. For love, true love, is nothing else but the joy of life, or life as the fullness of joy. Love is the indissoluble inner unity of life's fullness and intensity, or satisfaction. It is the union of the thirst for life and existence with joy, bliss, happiness. And that is why we understand that "God is love." We understand that "love is of God; and every one that loveth is born of God. . . . He that loveth not knoweth not God; for God is love" (1 John 4:7-8). "God is love; and he that dwelleth in love dwelleth in God, and God in him" (v. 16).

This is the essence of religious faith. This consciousness of the identity between the ultimate depths of being and absolute perfection, goodness, and bliss is that ultimate penetration into the mystery of being which saves us from the horror of life. In the human soul there live two fundamental, most profound feelings, forming as it were the two deepest roots with which the soul touches the absolute. One of them is the feeling of awe and trepidation before the profundity and immensity of *being*, before the bottomless abyss which surrounds us on all sides and is ready to swallow us at every moment. The other is the thirst for perfection, happiness, and peace, the desire to find an ultimate, luminous, warming refuge for the soul. The soul is torn apart by the opposition between these two feelings; it is thrown between two extremes: between a panicked horror before the immensity of being, and the inexpressible sweetness of the dream of salvation and peace. In our obscure and blind passions, in states of frenzy, in orgiastic intoxication with wine and sex, in explosions of rage, we experience the morbid, distorted unity of these antagonistic forces: the horror itself yields a momentary pleasure here, and the pleasure fills the heart with horror.

> There is intoxication in battle
> And in the somber abyss at the edge. . . .
> All things that threaten to destroy us
> Conceal inexpressible pleasures
> For the mortal's heart.[3]

But we can also find deliverance from this excruciating antagonism between the most profound forces of our spirit, from their morbid and unnatural confusion. We find it when — with the energy of our spiritual penetration into the ultimate depths of being and also as an undeserved gift from above — we suddenly discover that these two feelings diverge and oppose each other only because of their weakness and blindness. We discover that, in their ultimate depths, they are one and the same feeling, the perception of one and the same absolute principle. This higher, central, and unifying feeling which brings peace and tranquility into our soul is the feeling of *reverence*. Reverence is the immediate unity of fear and the joy of love. In it, we discover that the immeasurable depths of life bring to our soul not the blind and paralyzing feeling of insuperable horror, but the joyous consciousness of the *magnificence and inexpressible fullness of being;* and that the joy, happiness, and peace for which we yearn with such anguish are not a dream, not a flight from being, but the primordial ground of the most unsearchable depths of being. Reverence is the "fear of God," the fear which brings us the gift of tears of loving tenderness and the joy of perfect peace and of the final refuge. Reverence is fear overcome by love, and thoroughly permeated and transfigured by the latter. "There is no fear in love; but perfect love casteth out fear: because fear hath torment. He that feareth is not made perfect in love" (1 John 4:18).

In this direct feeling of reverence, which with inexpressible but perfect self-evidence reveals to us the ultimate mystery of being as the unity of being and perfection, of being and supreme joy, we have both conditions which are necessary if our lives are to be made meaningful. For in

---

3. These lines are from Pushkin's verse-play *The Feast during the Plague. Trans.*

this feeling, there is, first of all, directly revealed to us God's existence as the ultimate depth, as the unity of *all-powerfulness* and *all-goodness*. However paradoxical this conviction might be for the empirical consciousness and in the face of the facts of empirical life, it is for us a real, empirically verified, and therefore self-evident fact. And here, as in all other cases, our inability to reconcile this fact with other facts, our doubt as to how one can harmonize the imperfection and evil of the world's life with the reality of an all-good and all-powerful God — this inability and this doubt cannot disprove the fact itself (for it simply self-evidently is), but only poses new problems for our religious thought; and however difficult these problems may be to solve, we clearly know that the imperfection of the world is neither God's fault nor a result of His weakness, but has some other source which is in harmony with both His all-powerfulness and His all-goodness.

As for the second condition, together with this verification of God's existence, we also receive verification of the fact that we are in communion with Him, that He is close to us and accessible to us, and that therefore it is possible for us to attain the fullness and perfection of divine life. For God is not only *revealed* to us as another, higher, absolute principle which infinitely surpasses us; He is also revealed to us as the source and primordial ground of our personal being. We directly feel that we live and genuinely exist only insofar as we are in Him and by His power. He Himself is our being. Being His creations, creations "out of nothing," impotent and insignificant creatures, who, if not for His creative power, could at any moment fall into the abyss of non-being — at the same time we are conscious of ourselves as being in the "image and likeness of God," for He Himself shines not only for us but also within us, and His power is the foundation of our entire being. Furthermore, we are conscious of ourselves as the "sons of God"; we are conscious of Divine Humanity, of the connection of God with "man" (as the existent ideal proto-ground of every empirical, creaturely man), as the fundamental, primary fact of absolute being itself. We cannot identify ourselves with God; but neither can we separate ourselves from and oppose ourselves to Him, for at that moment we would disappear, turn into nothing.

And we begin to understand the mystery of the Divine Humanization and the Divine Incarnation. It was not enough for God to create the world and man. He also had to fill and permeate the world and man with Himself. Even before the creation of the world, His supra-eternal Word, the light and life of men, predetermined that full and perfect revelation of the Word which was manifested in the Divine Humanization. We have barely touched this mystery here; we have not yet disclosed it fully; but we understand its primary and necessary meaning. We know that, being impotent, corruptible, and vice-ridden beings, threatened every moment by destruction, by both physical and spiritual destruction — at the same time we are potentially eternal and potentially all-powerful, and we participate in the all-goodness by the eternal power of the God-Man: We know that Christ is with us always until the end of the world, and it depends only on us ourselves whether or not we become fully and wholly filled with Him, whether or not we become fully "clothed in Him," whether or not we grow intertwined with Him like a branch with a vine, and thus become nourished with the divine life, become "deified."[4] And here we also understand that, however difficult it might be for our thought to explain the contradiction between our empirical poverty and corruptibility and our metaphysical fullness and eternity, this "contradiction" can disprove the self-evident fact of our divinity just as little as the poverty and humble appearance of a born aristocrat can disprove his high origin, the nobility of his blood. Whatever difficulties might be associated with the explanation of this unnatural combination of traits in man, this combination *must* be possible, and its essential meaning is even immediately clear to us: In a certain sense, man is "fallen" and weak, and he himself is to blame for this fallenness and weakness, which, however, are connected with his freedom, that is, with his likeness to God.

God is the foundation of human life, its nourishment. He is that which human life needs if it is to become genuine life, if it is to disclose itself and become incarnate, if it is to acquire an unshakable foundation. In this interpretation, which is the Christian one, the existence of God as all-goodness and eternal life *coincides* with His proximity and accessibility to man, with man's ability to participate in Divinity and to fill his life with Divinity. Both conditions for the meaningfulness of life are given *at*

4. Frank is referring here to the patristic doctrine of "deification" or "theosis." *Trans.*

once — in the inseparable and inconfusible Divine Humanity.[5] In virtue of the Divine Humanity, God's work is my own work; and in giving my life to the service of God, in considering my entire life as a path to absolute perfection, I do not lose my life, I do not become a slave who serves someone else and thus is left with empty hands. On the contrary, I acquire my life for the first time in this service: ". . . whosoever will save his life shall lose it: but whosoever will lose his life for my sake, the same shall save it. For what is a man advantaged, if he gain the whole world, and lose himself, or be cast away?" (Luke 9:24-25). The commandment "Be ye therefore perfect, even as your Father which is in heaven is perfect" (Matt. 5:48), this unique, all-embracing commandment of our life, this commandment that we love God infinitely, with all the powers of our soul — this commandment is also the path to the attainment of the eternal and incorruptible treasure, to the enrichment of our soul. "The sabbath was made for man, and not man for the sabbath" (Mark 2:27), and our Path is not death, but Life. Truly, the Lord is right when He says, "My yoke is easy, and My burden is light" (Matt. 11:30).

But at the same time this is a path of struggle and renunciation — of the struggle of the Meaning of life against the meaninglessness of life, of the renunciation of blindness and emptiness for the sake of the light and richness of life. The action of God within us and thus the genuine realization of our life are everywhere opposed — both outside us and within us — by the meaningless forces of the world, which seek to destroy us. But the mysterious meaning of the Christian faith, a meaning so obvious to our hearts, teaches us that — behind the visible triumph of evil, death, and meaninglessness — is concealed the invisible but nevertheless certain victory of God over evil, death, and meaninglessness: ". . . the Jews require a sign, and the Greeks seek after wisdom: But we preach Christ crucified, unto the Jews a stumbling block and unto the Greeks foolishness" (1 Cor. 1:22-23). Our sensuous nature requires that, in the empirical, sensuous world, the certainty of God's victory over the blind powers of the world be proved to us. Otherwise, we do not wish to believe in Him, just as the Jews demanded that Christ descend from the cross before they would believe in Him. And our reason, our need for logical certainty, demands that it be

5. Frank is using the language of the Creed of Chalcedon. *Trans.*

philosophically *proved* to us that there is meaning in being, that God truly
is. But faith — since it is the certainty that invisible things exist, "the evidence of things not seen" (Heb. 11:1) — bears witness with self-evident certainty to that which diverges from the empirical facts of sensuous being
and surpasses all logical proof. "Blessed are they that have not seen, and
yet have believed" (John 20:29). This does not summon us to *blind* faith, to
slavish submission to authority, to infantile credulity; rather, it summons
us to spiritual vision, to the readiness to perceive and recognize the *higher*
evidence contrary to the *lower* evidence. After all, an analogous faith is re-
quired in other domains as well, including the domain of scientific knowledge. When, contrary to the evidence of visual perception and the insis-
tence of the authorities, Galileo affirmed that the earth revolves around
the sun, he too was sacrificing evidence of a lower order for the sake of the
relatively higher evidence of mathematical speculation.

The will to faith, firmness in upholding faith, is needed not in order
to blindly believe in what is impossible and meaningless. Rather, it is
needed in order to be firm in the consciousness that *higher evidence* has
priority over lower evidence, which psychologically may act more pow-
erfully on our nature, but logically has less justification than the higher
evidence. In essence, the lower evidence can never disprove the higher,
but can only, because of our weakness, illegitimately expel it from our
consciousness. Christianity teaches us this faith in the higher evidence
of the Divine Humanity, of God as the unity of goodness and life, of the
incarnation of Meaning in life and therefore the realizability of this
Meaning for us — *despite* the empirical meaninglessness of life and the
logical impossibility of "philosophically" clarifying its meaning. This
Christian revelation of God in the incarnation of God the Word reveals to
us *the ultimate evidence* which was perceived only obscurely by all the
great religious thinkers and which is obscurely felt by every human soul,
for the "soul is, by nature, a Christian," as Tertullian said. The absolute realization or incarnation of the Word, the Meaning of life, and therefore
the realizability of this Meaning in the life of each one of us, are self-
evidently certain; and this self-evident certainty preserves its validity *despite* the meaninglessness of empirical life.

Dostoevsky confesses somewhere that his love for Christ is so great
that, if the truth were against Christ, he would be on the side of Christ —

against the truth. To be sure, Dostoevsky's expression of this idea is purposely naïve, because the truth cannot be against the One Who is the absolute fullness of the living Truth. But what Dostoevsky means is easy to understand. The supreme and ultimate Truth is attained in Christianity through the *overcoming* of truth of a lower order (sensuous and logical truth) and is valid *contrary to it.* The truth discovered by Christianity — the truth of the Divine Humanity, based on the truth of the God-Man, on the living manifestation of God Himself — gives us certainty and, at the same time, demands from us the faith that the being who was crucified and died on the cross is the only begotten Son of God in whom resides the entire fullness of Divinity and who, by His resurrection, unshakably established the victory of life over death, of the meaning of life over its meaninglessness. The metaphysical all-powerfulness of the Good is manifested as certain in its empirical powerlessness: that which is impossible for men is not only possible but *exists* self-evidently with God and through God. And thus the conditions for the meaning of life are self-evidently realized, despite the empirical meaninglessness of life.

And we now understand that our complaints that life is meaningless, that it is impossible to find meaning in it, are, at least *in part,* simply illegitimate. Life *does have* meaning, and this meaning can be easily and simply realized for each one of us — for God is with us, within us.

> He is *here and now.* Amidst our random vanities,
> Within the turbid stream of life's anxieties
> You possess a wholly joyous secret:
> Evil is powerless. We are eternal. God is with us.[6]

Anyone who sees this and does not notice it has only himself to blame: his eyes are too near-sighted; his attention is too weak and unfocused. *Empirical* meaninglessness belongs to the very essence of the life of the world. This fact is just as indisputable and natural as the fact that fragments of pages torn from a book at random will not form a coherent whole, or that nothing is visible in the dark. Therefore, there is an internal contradiction in the very attempt to find absolute meaning in

---

6. These lines are from Vladimir Solovyov's poem "Immanuel." *Trans.*

empirical life, or to thoroughly "clarify its meaning." It is true that we have a legitimate desire and a righteous hope that everything in the world can be made meaningful and that everything that is meaningless will disappear. But the true meaning of this desire is found in the prayer "Let Thy kingdom come." And the true goal of this hope is found in the affirmation that God will be "all in all." Its meaning coincides with the ultimate task, with the expectation that the entire world will dissolve in God and stop existing as something separate from God, that is, as the world; with the expectation that there will be no more time. We find the guarantee for this hope in the resurrection of Christ. This is the hope for the ultimate transfiguration, which coincides with the end of the world. Whenever we are possessed by the obscure desire to make meaningful the empirical world as it is and to realize True Life and absolute meaning in worldly forms, we fall into a contradiction, we sacrifice — because we are impatient to see the realization of the meaning of life, the necessary conditions, i.e., the Divine conditions of its realizability. And, what is even worse, we *betray* — consciously or unconsciously — our higher goal: instead of attempting to attain genuine (i.e., absolute) meaning, we seek repose in some relative, worldly (i.e., meaningless) "meaning."

But the following objection is constantly and triumphantly raised by unbelievers: "Why was the existence of this meaningless world necessary? Why could God not create man and the world's life in such a way that they would be in Him at once and once and for always, in such a way that they would be permeated with His grace and His reason? Who needs our sufferings, our infirmities, our blindness, and why are they needed? But once they exist, life is nonetheless meaningless, and no justification can be found for it!" This objection of unbelievers often sows doubt in the minds of believers as well. But here one is forgetting that the ways of God are unfathomable, that, being all-good and all-knowing, God knows depths of goodness and reason which are inaccessible to us. Thus, the divine revelation in the book of Job and in the utterances of the prophets provides an answer to the unbelievers' objection. Barely having come into contact with the mysterious self-evidence for us of divine being, we already think that we have exhausted it, and we judge about it according to our human notions of goodness and reason. How do we know that that which *we* consider as goodness and reason are truly good and reasonable? After all, as we already know, our entire life passes in a series of errors, in a blind chase after illusory, deceptive goods!

But there is no need for us to limit ourselves to a simple reference to the unknowability for us of Divine Providence. For God, being unknowable, at the same time always reveals Himself to us, and all we have to do is learn to receive His revelation.[7] Do we not often see in life, in moments of spiritual clarity, that the calamities, sufferings, and evils that besiege us serve to further our good, are purifying and beneficent Divine punishments, manifestations of His love and wisdom? Are we not aware now too, if we are not totally blinded by our passions, whether individual or communal — are we not aware that that chaos of meaninglessness and evil which inundated our homeland, destroying our lives, has at the same time a certain profound religious meaning, that, evidently, it is for us the only true path to the religious — that is, the genuine — rebirth of our individual lives and of the life of our nation? But, guided by this example and by a multitude of similar examples, why is it that we cannot admit that, as a whole, the meaninglessness of the world is the same kind of path — necessary for us and therefore meaningful — to true life, even if we do not understand why this is so?

However, in one respect, and this is the chief one, we are even capable of understanding it. Somewhere in the Talmud, the fantasy of the Hebrew sages tells us of the existence of a holy land in which not only all people but also all of nature are absolutely obedient to God's commandments, so that, in fulfilling them, even rivers stop flowing on the Sabbath. Would we agree to having been created by God from the very beginning in such a way that, like these rivers, we would automatically, without reflection and without free rational choice, fulfill His commands? And in that case would the meaning of our life be realized? But if we did the good automatically and were rational by our very nature, if all the things around us automatically and with total compulsory certainty bore witness to God, to reason and the good — *then all things would at once become absolutely meaningless.* For "meaning" is a rational realiza-

---

7. Frank develops this thesis at length in his magnum opus, *The Unknowable: An Ontological Introduction to the Philosophy of Religion* (first published in Russian in 1939; English translation by Boris Jakim, Ohio University Press, 1983). *Trans.*

tion of life, and not the working of a wound clock; meaning is the genuine disclosure and fulfillment of the mysterious depths of our "I," and our "I" is inconceivable without freedom. This is because freedom and spontaneity require the possibility of our own initiative, and the latter presupposes that not everything runs smoothly and "automatically," that creative activity and spiritual power are needed to overcome obstacles. A kingdom of God which would be given "for free" and which would be predetermined once and for all would by no means be a kingdom of *God* for us, for in the true kingdom of God we must be free participants in the Divine glory, sons of God, and then we could not be slaves, we could not be tiny cogs in some sort of necessary mechanism. "The kingdom of heaven suffereth violence, and the violent take it by force" (Matt. 11:12), for in this effort, in this creative exploit, we find the necessary condition for *genuine* bliss, for the *genuine* meaning of life.

Thus, we see that the empirical meaninglessness of life against which man must struggle, against which he must maximally apply his will to creative exploit, his faith in the reality of Meaning — we see that this meaninglessness not only does not *hinder* the realization of the Meaning of life but that, in some enigmatic, not fully fathomable, but nonetheless empirically understandable way, it is actually the *necessary condition* for the realization of this Meaning. The meaninglessness of life is needed as an obstacle which must be overcome, for without the creative effort put into this overcoming, there is no real revelation of freedom; without freedom, all things become impersonal and lifeless. Without freedom, neither the life of *my "I"* itself nor the *life* of my "I" in its ultimate and genuine depths would be realized. For "wide is the gate, and broad is the way, that leadeth to destruction . . . [and] . . . strait is the gate, and narrow is the way, which leadeth unto life" (Matt. 7:13-14). Only one who lifts his cross upon his shoulders and follows Christ will acquire genuine life and the genuine meaning of life. And this is not a "sad necessity," based on some incomprehensible, random, and external imperfection of the world. Rather, this is a profound and mysterious inner law of human life, by virtue of which the very essence of life consists in freedom, in self-overcoming, in regeneration through dying and sacrifice — a law whose symbol is given in the "corn of wheat" (John 12:24) which, having fallen into the ground, will not come to life if it does not die. We stand here before the ultimate self-evident certainty, which is just as mysterious but also just as directly comprehensible to our heart as our entire life.

From this it is clear why the "meaning of life" cannot, so to speak, be found in a finished form, given once and for all as established in being, but why one can only strive to realize it. For the meaning of life is not *given;* it is *assigned as a task* that is to be accomplished. All things that are "finished," all things that exist outside of and independent of our will and of our life in general, are either dead or alien to us and suitable at best only as an auxiliary means for our *life.* But the meaning of life must, after all, be the meaning of *our* life; it must exist in our life and belong to the latter; it itself must be alive. Life, after all, is activity, creative works, spontaneous blossoming and ripening from inside, out of one's own depths. If we were able to *find* outside of ourselves a finished "meaning of life," it would not satisfy us; it would not be the meaning of our life, the justification of our own being.

The meaning of our life must be *within us;* we ourselves, *by our own life, must manifest this meaning.* Therefore, the search for the meaning of life is not an exercise of idle curiosity, not a passive observation of the things surrounding one, but an intense volitional immersion into one's depths, a genuine immersion — full of toil and deprivation and impossible without self-discipline — into the depths of being. "To find" the meaning of life is to act in such a way as to bring it into being; it is to exert one's inner powers to discover it and — more than that — to realize it. For, although its first condition — the existence of God — is the eternally existent proto-ground of everything else, but since this very existence is *life* and since we must participate in this existence, God being not the God of the dead but the God of the living, we must then — through the maximal exertion and disclosure of our being — "seek" the meaning of life and capture it in the creative process of its acquisition and our participation in it. Therefore, the search for the meaning of life is also always a *struggle* for meaning against meaninglessness; and it is not in idle reflection but only in the spiritual exploit of the struggle against the darkness of meaninglessness that we can attain meaning, establish it in ourselves, make it the meaning of our own life, and thus genuinely apprehend it or believe in it. Faith, since it is "the evidence of things not seen" (Heb. 11:1), is impossible without action; it itself is an intense inner action, which is necessarily manifested in an active transformation of our life, and for this reason "faith, if it hath not works, is dead" (James 2:17).

It is in this transformative action, and not in some theoretical reflection, that we can find the ultimate resolution of the aforementioned contradiction between true life and our entire empirical nature. We have seen that the evil and imperfection of our empirical nature is, for some unfathomable reason, necessary for the realization of the meaning of life: Without this evil and imperfection, *the freedom of spiritual exploit* would be impossible, and without this freedom the meaning of life would not be an authentic meaning, would not be what we are seeking. The intensity of the opposition between being and existence, between life and its evil and illusory simulacrum, expresses in some manner the very essence of our life as a way to perfection. This opposition must exist in order to be *destroyed.* For this contradiction, which theoretically cannot be totally removed, can and must be overcome in practice. It is true that it is not in our power (for we are weak, limited, and evil-poisoned beings) to accomplish the ultimate and conclusive triumph of true being and essential good. Only *true being itself* can accomplish this triumph; but after all, as we have seen with reference to the identity of perfection and being, and as Christian faith attests in the fact of Christ's redemption and resurrection, fundamentally this being *already has* this power, has already attained victory. But something does depend on us: it is in our power to *destroy in ourselves* that which contradicts this. It is in our power, as the Apostle says, to make it so that in us there live not we ourselves, but only the God-Man Himself, Christ.[8] This trampling of death (and therefore of the meaninglessness of life) by death,[9] following the example of Christ Himself; this voluntary self-annihilation of one's own creaturely being for the sake of the triumph in us of our divine being — this is the real, genuine overcoming of the fundamental excruciating contradiction of our life, the real attainment of the "Kingdom of Heaven." And it is in our power. Such is the final and definitive — not mental and theoretical but active and vital — overcoming of the world's meaninglessness by the truly existent meaning of life. The symbol of this overcoming is the cross, whose acceptance is the attainment of true life.

8. See Galatians 2:20. *Trans.*
9. Cf. the Paschal Hymn. *Trans.*

· VII ·

The Illumination of Life with Meaning

Thus, the search for the meaning of life is, strictly speaking, the illumination of life with meaning, the disclosure and introduction of meaning in life, of meaning which, without our spiritual activity, not only could not be found, but would not even exist in empirical life.

More precisely, faith as the search for and the apprehension of the meaning of life has two indissolubly connected aspects: the theoretical aspect and the practical one. The sought-for illumination of life with meaning is, on the one hand, an apprehension or *finding* of the meaning of life and, on the other hand, the active creation of this meaning, an effort of the will by which this meaning is "taken by force."[1] The theoretical aspect of the illumination of life with meaning consists in the fact that, having apprehended true being and its deepest and most genuine center, we thereby have life as a genuine whole, as a meaning-illuminated unity; and we therefore understand the meaningfulness of that which previously had been meaningless, since we only saw a fragment of it. Just as, in order to survey a place and to understand how it is situated, one must distance oneself from this place, step outside it, as on a high mountain *above it*, and thus truly see it for the first time — so, in order to understand life, one must go beyond it, so to speak, look at it from a height from which it can be seen as a whole. We will then become convinced that everything that had previously seemed meaningless to us was such

1. See Matthew 11:12. *Trans.*

only because it was a dependent fragment. When we do not perceive its genuine center, our individual personal life seems to us a plaything of the blind forces of fate, a point of intersection of meaningless accidents. But as we grow in self-knowledge, this personal life becomes a profoundly significant and coherent whole; and all its accidental events, all the blows of fate, acquire meaning for us; they all somehow fall into place, as necessary components, in that whole which we are called to realize.

The historical life of nations, which, as we have seen, presents to the empirical gaze a vista of the meaningless and chaotic collision of elemental forces, of collective passions or collective insanity, attesting only to the continuous collapse of all human hopes — this historical life of nations, when it is *contemplated in its profound depths,* becomes, like our individual life, coherent and rational, as if a "university course" in the self-revelation of Divinity being taken by our life. The profound German thinker Baader[2] was right when he said that, if we possessed the spiritual depth and religious insight of the compilers of the Sacred History, the entire history of mankind, the history of all nations and times, would be for us an uninterrupted continuation of the one Sacred History. It is only because we have lost the feeling for and the taste for the symbolic meaning of historical events that we take them solely in their empirical aspect: We take a sensuously distinct or rationally fathomable part as the whole of an event instead of glimpsing through this part the genuine, metaphysical whole. And it is only for this reason that the events of secular, "scientifically" knowable history seem to us a meaningless collection of blind accidents. Read — after a series of "scientific" histories of the French Revolution, after the Taines and Aulards [3] — *The French Revolution: A History* by Thomas Carlyle, who in the nineteenth century managed to preserve a small trace of the religious, prophetic understanding of life; and you will be convinced by a living example how, depending on the spiritual depth of the one who contemplates it, one and the same event can appear to be a meaningless and chaotic accident or can unfold into a somber but profoundly significant and meaningful tragedy of mankind,

2. Franz Baader (1765-1841) was an influential mystical philosopher and speculative theologian. *Trans.*

3. Hippolyte Taine (1828-1893) and Alphonse Aulard (1849-1928) were important French historians of the French Revolution. *Trans.*

revealing a rational coherence behind which we discern the wise will of Providence. And if we had eyes to see and ears to hear, then even today there would be Jeremiahs and Isaiahs in our midst, and we would understand that such events as the Russian Revolution, the collapse of the former glory and power of the Russian empire, and the diaspora of millions of Russians, have the same spiritual significance and display the same signs of Divine wisdom as the destruction of the Temple of Jerusalem and the Babylonian captivity. We would understand that, if the history of mankind appears to be the history of the successive collapse of all human hopes, this is the case only insofar as these hopes are blind and false, and violate the eternal commandments of God's wisdom. We would understand that, together with this, God's inviolable truth is affirmed in history; and that, taken together with its first, absolute beginning (the birth of man out of God's hands) and its necessary end (the completion of man's vocation on earth), history becomes an agonizing but rational and meaningful path of universal human life.

And finally, let us consider cosmic life. When it is taken as a self-enclosed whole, this life too, despite all its grandiosity, is nothing else but a meaningless play of blind forces. However, when it is considered in connection with its center, with the religious meaning of being, with the fate of Divine Humanity in the world, when it is perceived as a metaphysical whole, from its absolute beginning in the creation of the world to its yearned-for end in the transfiguration of the world — cosmic life, too, acquires a meaning, even if this is a meaning that we perceive only dimly. For in cosmic life, when it is apprehended in its indissoluble connection with eternal life, with God's supratemporal being, everything is a *symbol;* everything is a distorted and obscure reflection and manifestation — seen as if in a confused dream — of the great laws of spiritual being. Genuine insight into this matter is attained neither by the dominant mechanistic worldview (which, because of its blindness, sees in the world only a collection of dead levers, wheels, and screws), nor by the vitalistic worldview (which apprehends the cosmos as a living element), nor even by the ancient pantheistic conception which apprehends the world as a living being. Only Christian mystics and theosophists, such as Jacob Boehme and Baader, had the kind of profound insight that enables one to see in the world a visible likeness of invisible powers, and in its supposedly blind laws an embodiment of the rational laws of spiritual being. Then, viewing the world as the periphery of the absolute center, one discovers that the world is not at all meaningless, but that at each step it manifests to us traces of its origin from the absolute Wisdom, and that every phenomenon of nature is a symbol behind or in which the most profound meaning can be discovered.

Thus, everywhere, orientation toward the primary center of being, the opening of the veils which conceal from us the metaphysical depths of being, illuminates that which previously had been a total darkness, makes eternally significant that which previously had rushed past us in a chaotic vortex. Everywhere, the degree of penetration into the meaning of being depends on the spiritual acuity of the seeker after knowledge, on the degree to which *this seeker himself* is grounded upon the eternal Meaning of life. As the old Goethe said,

> *Isis zeigt sich ohne Schleier,*
> *Doch der Mensch, er hat den Star.*[4]

Alongside this theoretical illumination of life with meaning, there is another aspect of our spiritual re-education and immersion into the depths. We can call this other aspect the practical illumination of life with meaning, the active establishment of meaning in life, and the annihilation of its meaninglessness.

We know and foresee that, for the contemporary consciousness which is wholly oriented toward the world and active work in the latter, the theses developed above will appear too "detached from life," "lifeless." The opponents of the view of life we are presenting here would most likely say that, in this view, the fate of the world and all human works are dethroned, the enthusiasm for great works is suppressed, and man does not need to fulfill the duty of his life and ends up in a world-negating "quietism."

That the illumination of the world and of life with meaning is possible only through the detachment from the world in the sense of the denial of its claim to have autonomous and absolute significance, through

---

4. "Isis shows herself without a veil, but man has cataracts in his eyes." *Trans.*

the establishment of oneself in the supramundane, eternal, and truly all-embracing ground of being — this is simply a self-evident truth, a truth which in the domain of spiritual knowledge has the significance of an elementary axiom, without knowledge of which man is simply illiterate. And if this simple and elementary truth contradicts the "contemporary consciousness" or our prejudices based on passions, even the most noble ones, *then so much the worse for these passions!* But to reproach this understanding of life with quietism and to say that it preaches inactivity and passivity; to understand "detachment" to mean man's enclosedness within himself and a separation from life — this is a total misunderstanding, based on a failure to comprehend the true essence of the matter.

We have just seen that the spiritual orientation toward the primordial ground of being and the establishment of oneself in this ground do not make life meaningless for us, but, on the contrary, for the first time open for us that breadth of horizon which allows us to illuminate it with meaning. The deep immersion into oneself here, in the domain of knowledge, is not a closing up of the spirit, but rather its expansion, its liberation from all narrowness which conditions its blindness. But *the same relation* prevails also in the practical domain, in the sphere of active life. We have already seen that the search for the meaning of life is, strictly speaking, a *struggle* for this meaning, its creative affirmation through free inner activity.

It remains for us here to note one other aspect of the matter. We have already spoken about the fact that "God is love." The religious illumination of life with meaning, the disclosure of our rootedness in God and of our connectedness with Him, is in essence *the disclosure of the human soul,* the overcoming of the human soul's hopeless *self-enclosedness* in empirical life. True life is life in the all-embracing all-unity, the unceasing service of the absolute whole. We genuinely *find* ourselves and our life for the first time when we sacrifice ourselves and our empirical isolation and self-enclosedness, and establish our entire being in another — in God, as the original source of all life. But by doing so we connect ourselves — in the most profound, ontological manner — with all living things on earth and, first and foremost, with our neighbors and their fate. Let us recall Abba Dorotheus's famous trope: If we imagine that people are moving along the radii of a circle, the closer they come to the center of the circle, the closer they come to one another.

The commandment to love thy neighbor as thyself is not a supplementary commandment, externally added for some unknown reason to the commandment of infinite love for God, with all the powers of one's soul and with all one's thoughts.[5] The commandment to love one's neighbor as oneself flows from the commandment to love God as the necessary and natural consequence of the latter. The children of the one God — if they really are conscious of themselves as such and see in the Father the unique support and foundation of their lives — cannot fail to be brothers, cannot fail to love one another. A branch of the vine — if it is conscious of the fact that it lives only by the juices that flow in the entire vine and issue from its common root — cannot fail to feel the primordial unity of its own life with the life of all the other branches. *Love* is the foundation of all human life, its very essence; and if, in the world, human beings appear to themselves to be isolated and self-enclosed fragments of being which must assert themselves *at the cost* of other lives, by contrast, human beings who have found their genuine essence in the world-embracing unity are conscious of the fact that without love there is no life, and that the degree to which they truly *assert themselves* in their genuine essence is directly proportional to the degree to which they overcome their illusory self-enclosedness and find a foundation in the other. Outwardly, the human personality appears to be self-enclosed and separated from other beings, but, inwardly, in its depths, it communicates with all other beings, is fused with them in primordial unity.

Therefore, *the more deeply a human being goes inside himself, the more he will expand* and the more readily he will attain a natural and necessary connection with all other human beings, and with the entire life of the world as a whole. Thus, the usual opposition between immersion into one's inner depths and social interaction is superficial and based on a total misunderstanding of the structure of the spiritual world, of the genuine structure of being, invisible to the sensuous gaze. It is usually thought that people "socially interact" with one another when they ceaselessly run around, meet many people, read newspapers and publish

5. See Matthew 22:37-39; Mark 12:30-31; and Luke 10:27. *Trans.*

articles in them, attend meetings and give presentations at them, but that when a person immerses himself deep "in himself," he isolates himself from other people, loses his connection with them. That is an absurd illusion. At no time is a person so self-enclosed, so isolated, so abandoned by other people and himself forgetful of them, as when he totally devotes himself to external social intercourse, to external business dealings, to "society." And no one attains such loving attention, such sensitive understanding of another's life, such breadth of world-embracing love, as a hermit who, in prayer penetrating down into his own deepest depths, attains the primordial source of world-embracing universal life and of all-human Love, and lives in this source as in the unique element of his own being. A nonreligious person can gain some understanding of this relation if he considers the constant relation between *depth* and *width* in the entire sphere of spiritual culture: A genius — an individual who is immersed deeply into himself and goes his own way, predetermined by his own spiritual depths — turns out to be necessary and useful to all people, and even understandable by later generations and remote nations, because, out of his own depths, he extracts what is *common to all*. But a person whose life consists in the vanity of continuous external social interaction with a multitude of people, and who is ready to imitate people in all things, who wants to be "like everyone else" and to live together with everyone else, knowing only the outward surface of human life — such a person turns out to be an insignificant being, not needed by anyone and always alone.

This fundamental relation of spiritual being, this relation according to which the greatest human commonality and solidarity are found in the depths, has as its consequence the fact that genuine creative and productive work also is accomplished in the depths, and that precisely this profound inner activity is the common work accomplished by everyone not for himself alone, but for all. We have seen what this true and fundamental work of man consists in. It consists in the active grounding of ourselves upon the Proto-source of life, in the creative effort to pour ourselves into Him and Him into ourselves, to ground ourselves upon Him and thus actively to realize the meaning of life, to bring this meaning close to life and thereby to disperse the darkness of meaninglessness. It consists in the exploit of the directedness of our souls in prayer toward

God, in the ascetic exploit of the struggle with the murk and blindness of our sensuous passions, of our pride, our egotism, in the annihilation of our empirical being for the sake of resurrection in God. People usually think that a man who engages or attempts to engage in this type of activity either is "doing nothing" or, in any case, is egotistically concerned solely with his own fate, with his personal salvation, and is indifferent to people and their needs. They cite the counterexamples of "social activists," who are concerned with the organization of the fates of a multitude of people, or of soldiers, who give their lives for the good of their homeland, as individuals who truly act and, moreover, who act for the common good, for the good of others. But this entire argument is fundamentally false, since it is conditioned by total blindness, by the attachment of consciousness to the deceitful, superficial appearance of things.

First of all, what is genuine productive work? In the domain of material life, the science of political economy, or economics, distinguishes between "productive" and "non-productive" labor. It is true that, in this science, this distinction is highly relative, for not only those who directly "produce" goods, but also those who transport and sell them, as well as for servants of the state who are responsible for keeping order in society — in other words, all those who labor toward and participate in the common organization of life are equally necessary and are engaged in equally necessary work. Nevertheless, this distinction does have a certain serious meaning, and it is obvious that, if everyone begins to "organize" the economy and distribute goods, and no one produces them (as was the case at one time, and in part remains the case even today, in Soviet Russia), then everyone will die of hunger.

But the concept of productive and non-productive labor has apparently disappeared from the domain of spiritual life, even though this concept has an essential and decisive significance in this domain. In order to propagate ideas, in order to organize life in accordance with them, one must *have* them. In order to do good for people or to battle evil for the sake of good, it is, after all, necessary to have *good itself.* Here it is perfectly obvious that, without productive labor and accumulation of goods, life would be impossible, the distribution of goods in life and the utilization of them would be impossible. But who does the producing and accumulating here? Our notions about good are so vague that we think that good is a "relation between people," a natural quality of our behavior; we do not understand that good is *substantial,* that it is a reality which we must first of all seek to attain, which we must *possess* before doing good for other people with it. But *only* a spiritual activist[6] can attain and accumulate good; and each of us can attain and accumulate it only to the extent that we are spiritual activists and dedicate ourselves to inner spiritual activity. Therefore, the activity of prayer and ascesis is not a "fruitless occupation," unnecessary for life and based on the forgetting of life; rather, in the spiritual sphere, it is the sole productive work, the sole genuine production or acquisition of that nourishment without which all of us are condemned to a hungry death. This is not idle contemplation. This is difficult labor "in the sweat of one's face," but also a productive labor which enables the accumulation of goods; and this is therefore the fundamental and essential work of every man — the primary productive work without which all other human works would stop and become meaningless. If the mills are to have work to do, if the baker is to be able to bake and sell bread, it is necessary that grain be sowed and sprout, that the wheat grow and become filled with grains. Otherwise the mills will stop working, and we will have to nourish ourselves with chaff and grass. But we keep building new mills without end, which with great noise keep waving their wings in the wind; we are busy with the opening of new bakeries, with the organization of bread-distribution schedules; we are preoccupied with how not to offend or shortchange anyone, but we are forgetting about one trivial matter — about the sowing of the grain, the irrigation of the fields, and the growth of the wheat!

Thus, socialism concerns itself with the universal well-being of men, battling the "enemies of the people," holding meetings, publishing decrees, and organizing the social order — but not only does it not concern itself with the production of bread, but it even methodically destroys the crop fields, infesting them with weeds. After all, for socialism this "daily bread" is only an "opiate of the people" and the growing of good is a meaningless matter, with which only monks and other freeloaders con-

---

6. The term Frank uses here is *podvizhnik* (derived from *podvig,* meaning "ascetic exploit"), which in the Eastern Orthodox literature characterizes a person (often a monk or a hermit) engaged in the renunciation of fleshly things through the discipline of prayer and abstinence. *Trans.*

cern themselves out of idleness! And then there is the American tempo of life: Millions of people in America and Europe are in a state of endless hustle-and-bustle, conducting all kinds of business and seeking to become rich; but in the final analysis all that these people can create together with their indefatigable labors is a desert in which they are tormented by the intense heat and perish from spiritual thirst. Or consider the political fever that has infected orators at meetings and editorial writers for newspapers: their preaching of justice and righteousness is so intense and frenzied that the souls of the preachers as well as of the listeners or readers are totally emptied, and no one knows anymore what he is living for, or where the truth and good of his life reside. All of us, we people of the present day, live more or less in a crazy society,[7] which, like Russia in the years of the Revolution, exists only by *squandering* the goods which were once imperceptibly produced by our predecessors in tranquil, invisible workshops.

Each one of us, whatever other work he might be engaged in, should devote a portion of his time to the most important work — to the accumulation inside himself of powers of good, without which all other works become meaningless or harmful. Our Russian-émigré politicians like to bring up St. Sergius of Radonezh and to point out approvingly that this great saint blessed the army of Dimitry of the Don and gave him two monks from his monastery.[8] This is the only aspect of the work of St. Sergius recalled by our politicians, but they forget to mention that this political work of the saint was preceded by decades of an unceasing labor of prayer and ascesis, that it was *this* labor that enabled the acquisition of the spiritual riches which nourished the Russian people for many centuries, and which continue to nourish them, and that without this la-

---

7. Frank is referring to the situation in Europe in the early 1920s. *Trans.*

8. In 1380 the army led by the Moscow Prince Dimitry Ivanovich defeated the Tatar hordes of Khan Mamai. The battle, which took place on Kulikovo Plain near the bank of the Don, is considered to be the most important victory in Russian history, a turning point in the struggle to liberate Russia from the Tatar yoke. According to some stories, Dimitry Ivanovich paid a visit to Sergius of Radonezh (considered by posterity to be the greatest Russian saint), the abbot of the Trinity Monastery near Moscow. Sergius, as these stories have it, ordered two of his monks to follow the prince during the campaign. It is an established fact that Abbot Sergius sent a message to the prince calling on him to take up arms against the enemies. *Trans.*

bor (as the perspicacious Russian historian Kliuchevsky pointed out) the Russian people would never have acquired the strength to rise in battle against the Tatars.

We rush to battle evil, to organize our lives, to do the present, "practical" work, but we forget that the primary requisite for this is the powers of good, which we must know how to grow and accumulate in ourselves. Inner religious activity, prayer, the ascetic struggle with oneself — this is the imperceptible labor of human life which lays the very foundation of the latter. This is the fundamental, primary, unique, genuinely productive human work. As we have seen, all human strivings — in the final analysis, in their ultimate essence — are strivings for *life*, for fullness of satisfaction, for the acquisition of light and the stability of being. But precisely for this reason all external human works, all the means of the external organization of life, are based on inner work — on the illumination of life with meaning through spiritual activity, through the growing of the forces of good and righteousness in oneself, through the active and vital participation of man in the Proto-source of life — God.

Furthermore, although in order to live — both in the physical and in the spiritual sense — every man *himself* must breathe and nourish himself, and cannot live only at the expense of the labor of others, it does not follow from this, as is usually thought, that invisible, silent, inner activity is work only for oneself, that in this activity men are isolated from one another, each being occupied solely with his own egotistical work. On the contrary, we have already seen that men are isolated from one another on the surface but are connected in their depths, and that for this reason every immersion into one's depths is therefore an expansion, an overcoming of the barriers that separate men from one another. Our era, which is poisoned by materialism, has totally lost the idea of the universal, cosmic, or — so to speak — magical power of prayers and spiritual activity. We need the obscure and risky miracles of occult phenomena and spiritistic séances in order to believe that, as a "rare exception," the spirit can act at a distance, that human hearts are connected by other means than through the action of the sounds emitted from the mouth of one person reaching the eardrum of another.

In reality, spiritual power is always supra-individual, and it always establishes an invisible connection between human beings. The experience of prayers and of spiritual activity confirms this in a myriad of particular examples, and discloses it at once as a general relation. A solitary hermit in his cell, not seen and not heard by anyone, accomplishes a work that, at the same time, has an immediate effect on life as a whole and touches all people. He accomplishes a work that not only is more productive but also is more *communal*, involving and influencing more people, than the work of the most skillful political orator or editorial writer. Of course, we, who are weak and unskillful ordinary laborers in the field of spiritual being, cannot count on *such* an effect of our inner work. But, if we are not conceited, can we count on greater results in the domain of our external activity in life? The fundamental relation here remains the same: that which is impossible for man is possible for God, and no man knows in advance to what extent he is capable of helping other people with his prayer, with his search for truth, with his inner struggle with himself. In any case, this fundamental human work of the active illumination of life with meaning, of the growing in oneself of the powers of good and righteousness, is not just the singular work of each one of us in isolation; rather, according to its very essence, according to the nature of that domain of being in which this work is being accomplished, it is a common and communal work in which all men are connected in God, and all are for one and one is for all.

This is the great and unique work by means of which we are actively realizing the meaning of life and by virtue of which something essential is really being accomplished in the world — namely, the regeneration of the inner fabric of the world, the defeat of the forces of evil, and the filling of the world with the forces of good. This work, a genuinely metaphysical one, is in general possible only because it is by no means merely a human work. The role of man's work here is to prepare the soil, whereas the growth from the soil is accomplished by God Himself. This is a metaphysical, Divine-human process, in which man is only a co-participant; and this is precisely why, in this process, the foundation of human life on its genuine meaning can be realized.

This makes clear the absurdity of the illusion in which we find ourselves when we think that, in our external activity, in work that occurs in time and participates in the temporal change of the world, we can realize something absolute, attain the realization of the meaning of life. The meaning of life consists in the rootedness of life in the eternal; this meaning is realized when the eternal principle is manifested inside us and around us; this meaning demands the immersion of life in this eternal principle. Only insofar as our life and our labor make contact with the eternal, live in and are permeated by the eternal, can we in general count on the attainment of the meaning of life. But, in time, all things are fragmented and fluid; all things that are born in time deserve, according to the poet, to perish in time. Insofar as we live only in time, we also live only *for time:* we are swallowed up by time, and it inexorably carries us away together with all our work. We live in a part, separated from the whole; in a fragment, which cannot fail to be meaningless. Let it be the case that, as participants in the world, we are condemned to this life in time; let it be the case (as will be clarified below) that we are even *obliged* to participate in this life in time, but in *this* work of ours, even when it is most successful, we can attain only relative values and by no means can this work illuminate our life with meaning. As nothing more than events of historical life, as nothing more than phenomena of the temporal world, great political, social, or even cultural changes do not accomplish the metaphysical *underground* work which we need; they do not bring us close to the meaning of life. Similarly, all of our own works, even the most important and necessary ones, accomplished by us, as it were, *inside* the car of the train in which we are traveling — all these works do not bring us a step closer to the goal toward which we are moving.

In order to change and correct our life in a *substantial* way, we must perfect our life all at once and as a *whole*; but in time it is given only in parts and, living in time, we live only in a small and evanescent fragment of life. The work done upon life as a whole is precisely spiritual work; it is activity that brings us into contact with the eternal, as given at once and as a whole. Only this underground work, invisible to the world, brings us into contact with those depths which contain pure gold, genuinely necessary for life. The sole work which illuminates life with meaning and therefore has absolute meaning for man is therefore nothing else but active co-participation in the Divine-human life. And we understand the words of the Savior, when to the question "What shall we do?" He responds, "This is the work of God, that ye believe in him whom he hath sent" (John 6:28-29).

On Spiritual and Worldly* Work

B ut what should our attitude be toward all other human works, toward all the interests of our empirical life, toward all the things that surround us and fill our ordinary life? Should the illumination of life with meaning be gained at the cost of renouncing all earthly things, the entire empirical content of life? Should we consider meaningless such things as love, family, the need to earn one's daily bread, as well as such goods which we usually consider objectively valuable and to which many men dedicate their lives, that is, such goods as science, art, justice in human relationships, the destiny of one's homeland, and so on. Are these things only an illusion, will-o'-the-wisps, the chase after which destroys our life for no reason and which we must therefore simply renounce? In this case, is the meaning of life not gained at the cost of the terrible impoverishment of life, and is this not too high a price to pay?

These questions are posed to us by our pagan nature, which we have not yet overcome. And our *first* answer must be as follows: Anyone who does not understand that the "meaning of life" is a good which surpasses all other human goods, that the genuine acquisition of this meaning is the acquisition of a treasure which immeasurably enriches the human soul, and — more than that — that this meaning is the *unique* real (and

---

*Here, *worldly* is taken to mean "of the world," as contrasted to "heavenly" or "eternal." *Trans.*

not imaginary or illusory) good and therefore cannot be bought at "too high a price" — that person has not yet known true thirst, and these words are not being written for him. Anyone whose heart does not respond with profound inner trembling to these words of the Savior: "Whosoever will save his life shall lose it: but whosoever will lose his life for my sake, the same shall save it. For what is a man advantaged, if he gain the whole world, and lose himself, or be cast away?" (Luke 9:24-25); anyone who does not understand that "the kingdom of heaven is like unto treasure hid in a field: the which when a man hath found, he hideth, and for joy thereof goeth and selleth all that he hath, and buyeth that field" or "like unto a merchant man, seeking goodly pearls: who, when he had found one pearl of great price, went and sold all that he had, and bought it" (Matt. 13:44-46) — that person is not yet ready to *seek* the meaning of life and therefore will never agree with those who seek it; and even less will he agree to the conditions under which it can be found. Without sacrifice and renunciation, one cannot find the meaning of life, or (what is the same thing) genuine life. That, as we already know, is the inner law of spiritual being; and that there cannot be too great a sacrifice here is clear to anyone who understands what this matter is about.

There is one conclusion of our reflections which is unshakably certain: in order to seek and to find the *absolute good,* one must first of all renounce the error that sees the absolute itself in what is relative and particular, that is, one must understand that everything in the world is meaningless *unless it is connected* with the genuinely absolute good. However often our soul, vacillating between two worlds, might return to the notion — more natural and easier for it — that the "true" and "real" satisfaction of the human soul consists in riches, glory, earthly love, or even in such suprapersonal goods as the happiness of mankind, the good of the homeland, science, art, and so on, whereas everything else is a foggy and illusory "metaphysics" — when it awakens from this notion, it again understands and (if it remains true to itself) cannot fail to understand that all this is corruption and vanity, and that the only thing it genuinely needs is the meaning of life, contained in the genuine, eternal, illuminated, and tranquil life. The relative and particular will always remain only the relative and particular, is always necessary only for something else, namely, the absolute, and is easily given up or at least should be given up for the latter. This hierarchy of values — this *primacy* of goal over means, of the fundamental over the secondary and derivative — must be unshakably affirmed in our soul once and for always and protected against the dangers of obscuration and vacillation to which it is always subject when we are possessed by *passion,* even the purest and most elevated passion. Life is illuminated with meaning only by the renunciation of its empirical content; we find a firm and genuine support for life only outside this content. Only by going beyond the limits of the world can we find the eternal foundation on which it is grounded. In abiding in the world, we are captured by it; and together with it we stagger and whirl in a meaningless vortex.

Nevertheless, we cannot limit ourselves to such a purely negative conclusion, for it is one-sided. This is because the meaning of life — once it is found through renunciation and sacrifice — at the same time, in the ultimate depths of being, illuminates *all* of life with meaning. Like a "pearl of great price," for which all other property is readily sacrificed, the Kingdom of Heaven is also like a leaven which leavens "three measures of meal," and like a grain of mustard seed which grows into an enormous shade tree. Expressing ourselves abstractly, we can say that the absolute is found by opposing it to the relative; it is outside and above the latter; but it would not be the absolute if at the same time it did not permeate and embrace all that is relative. No earthly human work, no earthly interest, can *illuminate life with meaning;* and in this respect all earthly works and interests are totally meaningless. But when life is already *illuminated with meaning* by another principle, that is, by its own ultimate depths, then it is illuminated with meaning wholly and, consequently, all of its content is illuminated with meaning. The light cannot be found in darkness, and the light is opposite to darkness; but the light illuminates the darkness.

To tear God away from the world, to enclose oneself within God and protect oneself from the world by despising it, would be totally false. It would contradict the Christian consciousness and the genuine structure of being. For God, who surpasses the world and is supramundane, created the world and manifested Himself in it. In the Divine Incarnation He Himself poured His powers into the world; and the truth of Christianity, in which we have recognized the true attainment of the meaning of life, is not a doctrine that proclaims the transcendent God, detached from the world, but a doctrine of the Divine Incarnation and the Divine Humanity, of the unity — without separation and without confusion[1] — of God and man and, therefore, of God and the world (since the essence of the world is in man). All of human life, illuminated by its connection with God and grounded through this connection, is justified. All of human life can take place "to the glory of God," luminously and meaningfully. The sole condition for this is the requirement that *man not serve the world,* that he "love not the world, neither the things that are in the world" (1 John 2:15) as ultimate, self-sufficient goods, but that he view his worldly life and the whole world as a means and an instrument of God's work, that he use his worldly life to *serve* the absolute good and genuine life. Life as pleasure, power, and riches, as intoxication with the world and with oneself, is meaninglessness; whereas life as *service* is Divine-human work and, consequently, wholly illuminated with meaning. And every illusory human good — love for a woman, riches, power, family, homeland — when it is used as *service,* as a path to true life, when it is illuminated by rays of the "serene light,"[2] loses its vanity, its illusoriness, and acquires eternal — that is, genuine — *meaning.* Christ blessed the marriage in Cana of Galilee; He commanded that the tribute be paid to Caesar — on condition that Caesar was not confused with God. Aside from the absolute demand to "bring forth fruits worthy of repentance," John the Baptist — in response to the question "What shall we do?" — commanded the people to share their clothing and their food with those who had none, the publicans to "exact no more than that which is appointed" them, and the soldiers to "do violence to no man, neither accuse any falsely; and be content with your wages" (Luke 3:8-14).

Nevertheless, something is still unclear. After all, it is said, "My kingdom is not of this world" and "Love not the world, neither the things that are in the world." The service of God is, after all, the renunciation of the world, for one cannot serve two masters at the same time: God and

1. Here, Frank is using the language of the Creed of Chalcedon. *Trans.*
2. This is a term used in Eastern Orthodox monasticism to describe the illumination of the ascetic's soul by God's grace. *Trans.*

mammon. But, then, how is worldly service possible, the justification of worldly life through its connection with God?

By his nature, man belongs to two worlds — to God and to the world. Man's heart is the point of intersection of these two forces. He cannot serve both of these forces at once, and he must have only one master — God. But God is also the Creator of the world, and the world is justified through God and in God. One who can renounce the world wholly, one who can renounce all things in the world that are not in harmony with God and are not divine, and go directly to God — this one acts righteously: By the shortest and truest — although most difficult — path, he finds the justification and meaning of his life. That is how hermits and saints go to God. But there are those who have another vocation. They have to go to God and realize the meaning of their life *by two paths at once:* To the extent they are able, they must attempt to go directly and steadily to God and to allow His power to grow in them; *and at the same time,* they must attempt to go to Him through the modification and perfection of the worldly forces in and around themselves, through the adaptation of all these forces to the service of God. That is the path of the worldly servant of God. And on this path there necessarily and *legitimately* arises that duality by virtue of which the renunciation of the world must be combined with a loving participation in it, with the effort to bring the world close, by its own means, to the eternal truth.

In other words, there exist a true renunciation of the "world" and a false one. The true renunciation consists in the active suppression in oneself of worldly passions, in emancipation from them, in a clear and actively confirmed realization that all earthly goods are illusory. The false renunciation consists in the de facto utilization of life's goods, in enslavement by the world, combined with the desire not to participate actively in the world's life and not to come into external contact with its sinfulness. Those who practice such an illusory renunciation, consisting in an attempt to abstain from external participation in the sins of the world while using its goods, actually commit a *greater* sin than those who, participating in the world and burdening themselves with its sinfulness, seek — in this participation — to overcome this sinfulness in the end. War is an evil and a sin, and a monk and hermit is right when he abstains from participation in it. But he is right because he never uses the fruits of war, because he does not need the political state which is waging the war and all that the state gives to men: Those who are ready to use the fruits of war, those who still need a state, bear responsibility for the destiny of the state and, sinning together with the latter, they sin less than those who wash their hands of the matter and shift the sin to others. Sexual love is imperfect love, and virginity is the perfect state of human beings, leading to God truly and by the shortest path. But, according to the Apostle, "it is better to marry than to burn" (1 Cor. 7:9); and therefore marriage is the worldly path of the purification of the fleshly life, expressing — albeit in an imperfect and distorted way — the mysterious connection between man and woman, which is a symbol of God's connection with humanity. Concerns about food and clothing are an expression of human weakness and human disbelief. Legitimately free of such concerns are those who, like Seraphim of Sarov,[3] can find nourishment in the grass of the field; and each one of us, insofar as he is able, must attempt to liberate himself from these concerns. But insofar as we are not free of them, diligence in work is better than idleness, and a hardworking family man sins less than an idler and egotist who is indifferent to the needs of those close to him. Violence done to people, even in combatting criminals, is a sin and an expression of our weakness; but truly free of this sin are not those who look indifferently upon crime and are coldly passive in relation to the evil it causes, but only those who are able to enlighten evil will and to stop the criminal by the power of God's light. Those sin *less* who use violence to stop a criminal than those who indifferently wash their hands in the face of the crime.

Generally speaking, one must remember that a man is legitimately free of worldly toil and worldly struggle only if, in his spiritual life, he is accomplishing an *even more arduous toil,* waging an *even more dangerous and difficult struggle.* Just as grace does not revoke the law but fulfills it, and only those have the right not to think about the law who graciously accomplish *more* than the law requires — so moral obligations imposed by the very fact of our participation in life can be neglected only by those who impose even more arduous obligations upon themselves. Human

---

3. Seraphim of Sarov (1759-1833), saintly ascetic and elder, is generally considered to be the greatest modern Russian saint. *Trans.*

life in its very essence is toil and struggle, for it is realized, as we already know, only through self-overcoming, through the active re-education of oneself and the effort to absorb into oneself one's Divine Proto-source. Therefore, false and illegitimate is the sentimentally idyllic desire to "escape" from the vanity of the world, from its cares and alarms, in an effort to live peacefully and to innocently enjoy a tranquil life in solitude. Such a desire is based on the unexpressed conviction that the world outside me is full of evil and temptations, but that a man in his intrinsic nature, that is, I myself, is innocent and virtuous. This conviction, originating with Rousseau, is the basis of all Tolstoyanism.

But, in reality, I bear this evil world *in myself* and therefore cannot escape anywhere from it. And as the experience of hermits has shown, one needs an enormous amount of courage and force of will, of spiritual effort, to overcome the great many temptations that arise in solitude. The hermit's life is not a life of idle contemplation, not a peaceful idyll, but the severe life of an ascetic, full of cruel tragedy and of a creative energy of will of which we can have only a dim idea. Seraphim of Sarov, who spent a thousand days and nights kneeling on a rock and who said that the goal of this ascesis was "to torment the one tormenting me" — Seraphim here revealed, of course, immeasurably more patience and courage than the most heroic soldier in a war. He battled the entire world, in himself, and he was therefore free of external battle with the world. Those who cannot do the same, those who live in the world and in whom the world lives, are therefore obligated to bear the burden that the world imposes on us. They are obligated to help establish in the world principles and relations which bring the world close to its Divine Protoground, even if these principles are embodied in imperfect, sinful, worldly forms.

In essence, this false idyllic asceticism is based on the notion (borrowed from the purely sensuous domain) of the separateness of human beings or of the possibility of their separation by purely physical means — by means of "isolation" from other human beings. But, as we already know, in the depths, in the primordial ground of their life, human beings are not separated. Rather, they are connected in a fundamental manner; they are embraced by one common element of being — be it the element of good or the element of evil. Every human being bears responsibility for all, because he suffers from one common evil and is healed by one common good. Therefore, only he has the right to physically separate himself from other human beings and not to participate in their worldly fate who is battling in himself against the very root of worldly evil and growing in himself the one, common, universally beneficial, substantial good. But anyone who still finds himself in opposition to others, who has his own personal sufferings and joys — this person still depends on the world, still lives in the world, that is, outwardly too he participates in the collective life of the world (even if he has renounced such participation in a physical and visible manner); and therefore he is responsible *for this life,* is obliged to participate in the obligations imposed by it. He is obliged to accomplish the maximal good, or to achieve the minimal overall sinfulness in the given, totally concrete situation, determined by the given conditions of human life.

In consequence, one who has understood the meaning of life will find it necessary to connect each step of life with the absolute Proto-ground of life. Obligations before the world and other people arise — the obligations of a good citizen and of a good person in general. And if in fulfilling these obligations one inevitably participates in the world's sinfulness (for all empirical, worldly life is full of imperfection and sinfulness), he must understand that he *nonetheless* bears this sinfulness within himself, that he nonetheless participates in it even if he remains passive and distances himself from people. But in the latter case he does not redeem the sinfulness by moral work, which in the final analysis flows from love for people, as a direct expression of love for God. It is said, "Love not the world, neither the things that are in the world. If any man love the world, the love of the Father is not in him. For all that is in the world . . . is not of the Father, but is of the world. And the world passeth away, and the lust thereof; but he that doeth the will of God abideth for ever" (1 John 1:15-17). But the same apostle — the apostle of love — also said, "If a man say, I love God, and hateth his brother, he is a liar: for he that loveth not his brother whom he *hath seen,* how can he love God whom he *hath not seen?*[4] And this commandment have we from him, that he who loveth God love brother also" (1 John 4:20-21). This love for the brother that one

4. The italics are Frank's. *Trans.*

has "seen" and the obligation to lighten his suffering and to help him in his battle against evil and in his striving for good, this love for living human beings in their sensuously empirical concreteness, realized by external empirical actions in the world, is the source of all our worldly obligations. And this love connects our direct relation to God, our spiritual work of the illumination of life with meaning, with our activity in the world by worldly means.

But, in general, what can be done in the world by worldly means? What does this mean from the point of view which interests us, from the only point of view that can interest every awakened human being who has understood the meaninglessness of empirical life as such — that is, from the point of view of the illumination of life with meaning, of the realization in it of essential good and true life, of the striving for its "deification"? It is necessary to achieve a clear understanding of this, free of all ambiguity.

As we have already said, in the genuine, metaphysical sense, man has only one work: that about which the Savior reminded Martha, when He told her that she was troubled about many things, but should be troubled about the one thing that is needful (Luke 10:41-42). This is spiritual work, the growing in oneself of substantial good, the effort to achieve life with Christ and in Christ, the battle with all the empirical forces that seek to prevent this. No external activity, not even the most energetic activity and useful in other respects, can create or accomplish even the smallest amount of good in the world; and not even the most intense and successful external battle with evil can destroy a single atom of evil in the world. In general, good is not created by human beings; it is only grown by them — when they prepare in themselves the soil for it and care for its growth. It is the power of God that creates the good and makes it grow. For good is precisely God. And the only way to really *destroy* evil is to expel it with essential good, for evil, being emptiness, is destroyed only by being *filled;* and being darkness, it is dispersed only by light. Like emptiness and darkness, evil cannot be crushed, annihilated, destroyed by any direct means — for it slips away from all such attempts. The way to get rid of it is to make it disappear, in the same way that wax melts in fire, darkness is dispersed by light, and emptiness disappears when it is filled. In this genuine, essential sense, good and evil live only in the depths of the human soul, in human will and human thoughts; and it is only in these depths that the battle between them is waged and evil can be expelled by good.

But man is also a corporeal — and thus a cosmic — being. His will has two ends: the inner one, penetrating down to the metaphysical depths, in which the true, genuine work is accomplished; and the outer one, manifested in external activity, in one's manner of life, in social arrangements and relationships between people. This external life, or the life of this outer and outward-directed end of human will, is not an indifferent matter for the life of the inner essence of the soul, although it can never replace this life and accomplish its work. For this inner essence of the soul, the external life plays a dual auxiliary role. On the one hand, by disciplining and organizing the external life, one can indirectly act upon the inner essence of the will, facilitating the work of this inner essence; however, one can also weaken the inner will and hinder its work by unchaining the external life. On the other hand, the general external orders of life and that which occurs in the latter can help or harm the spiritual being of man. In the first case, one can say that all training of the will begins with its external disciplining and is sustained by the latter: it is useful for a man to rise early, to work at something even if it is insignificant, to organize his life, to abstain from excesses. This leads to a series of external norms of conduct, to which we ourselves must adhere and which we must teach others. And work done to establish such an external organization of life, of one's own life and that of others, indirectly facilitates the fundamental task of our life. On the other hand, good, once it is realized, is manifested outwardly and is beneficial for its entire environment; evil too exists and is manifested in the destruction and crippling of the life around it; like a magnet, evil attracts to itself all the things around it and forces these things to manifest themselves and spoil life; and, in this manner, evil can hinder our inner spiritual life and — in proportion to our weakness — even make it impossible.

Therefore, *the protection of good* on the outside, the establishment of favorable external conditions for its outward manifestation and action, and *the restraining of evil,* the limitation of the freedom of its manifestation, constitute the most important auxiliary activities of human life. Each of these activities is, on the one hand, a work of law, insofar as it is accomplished and protected by the state, a work of the normalization of the general, "social" conditions of human life; and on the other hand, each of them is the daily work of each of us in our personal life, in our life with family and friends, in our business dealings, and so on. Thus, the external training of will and the facilitation of its inner work through its disciplining in actions and behavior, and second, the establishment of general conditions protecting the already-realized forces of good and restraining the ruinous actions of evil — that is the essential content of man's worldly work. Whether it is a question of work that feeds us, of our relations to other people, of family life and the upbringing of children, or of our diverse social responsibilities and needs — everywhere, the work here is reducible in the final analysis either to our external education, both individual and collective, which is indirectly useful for our free and inner spiritual re-education; or to work devoted to the protection of good and the restraining of evil.

Two reciprocally opposite and therefore similar errors, two misunderstandings of the fundamental structure of being, present themselves here as obstacles to the establishment of a healthy and rational relation to life. Confusing external life with inner life, not understanding the difference between the protection of good and the restraining of evil on the one hand and between the realization of good and the destruction of evil on the other, some people assert that all external social and state activity is useless and evil; whereas others, on the contrary, consider such activity to be equivalent to inner activity and believe that, through it, they can realize good and destroy evil. Tolstoyans[5] and partisans of the external works of law and the state share *the same error*: they confuse essentially creative work with auxiliary and mechanical work, the inner with the outer, the absolute with the relative. To reject the relative because it is not absolute is an error, and it is equally an error to raise it to the significance of the absolute. Both of these things signify a failure to understand the difference between the absolute and the relative, a failure to recognize the relative legitimacy of the relative. To do either of these things is to violate the commandment to "render . . . unto Caesar the things which are Caesar's, and unto God the things that are God's" (Matt. 22:21; cf. Mark 12:17, Luke 20:25).

5. Tolstoyans, the followers of Leo Tolstoy, considered law and the state to be evil. For them, all good emanated from man's soul. *Trans.*

Tolstoyans are *right* when they say that by violence one cannot create good and destroy evil, that no externally mechanical activity of the state or of law can realize the most important thing: the inner acquisition in oneself of good, the free inner education of human beings, the growth of love in human life. But they are *not right* when, for this reason, they consider this whole sphere of life and activity to be unnecessary and ruinous. If it is impossible to create good on this path, it is possible and necessary to *protect* it; if it is impossible to destroy evil, it is possible to *restrain* it and not allow it to destroy life. No punishment, however severe, including capital punishment, can destroy a single atom of evil in the world, for evil in its being cannot be grasped by external measures. But does it follow from this that we should allow murderers and other criminals to freely ruin and cripple life, without having the right to restrain them? Vladimir Solovyov[6] spoke justly when he said that the state exists not to establish heaven on earth, but to keep *hell* from being established on earth.

On the other hand, the partisans of social and political power are *right* when they affirm that it is the obligation of every citizen to concern himself with the improvement of the general, social conditions of life, to actively battle evil, and to assist in — if necessary, with a sword in his hands — the establishment of good. But they are *not right* when they think that, with a sword in one's hands, one can destroy evil and create good, that *evil and good themselves* are created and battle against each other in political activity and struggle. Evil is destroyed by the creation of good. And good is created only by spiritual work and by the actualization of such work: the loving union of people. Good has never been realized by any decree; it has never been created even by the most energetic and rational social activity; quietly and imperceptibly, apart from the noise, vanity, and struggle of social life, good grows in the souls of human beings, and *nothing* can replace this profound organic process, created by superhuman powers. And, as we have indicated, evil has never been destroyed by any punishments or acts of violence. On the contrary, when violence considers itself to be all-powerful and dreams of really *destroying* evil (and not only of restraining it, of protecting life against it), it always multiplies evil. This is

---

6. Vladimir Solovyov (1853-1900), the greatest Russian philosopher, had a profound influence on S. L. Frank. *Trans.*

attested by the effects of all terror (whatever its source or alleged purpose), of all fanatical attempts to destroy evil in the persons of the villains themselves. Such terror engenders around itself a new embitterment, blind passions of vengeance and hatred. "Apoliticism," contempt for social life, the unwillingness to dirty oneself with participation in it — this is, of course, a product of inconsistent thinking or "indifferentism," while religious apoliticism is a type of hypocrisy. On the other hand, political fanaticism and the cult of violence and hatred engendered by it are a blind idolatry, a betrayal of God, a worshipping of the statue of Caesar.

That which we have said about the attitude toward political and state power is applicable to all external, worldly activity, whether it be economic activity, concern for the order and well-being of one's household, the external education of people, the technological improvement of life or even scientific work, or the selfless activity of material assistance rendered to one's neighbor. All such activity, when it is put in its proper place, namely, as an auxiliary means externally facilitating the fundamental spiritual work of the deification of life, accomplished in the name of Christ and with Christ — all such activity not only is legitimate but is obligatory for all those who are not capable of totally suppressing in themselves the influence of the world. But when such activity is performed as an absolute work and is meant to replace the fundamental inner work of spiritual regeneration, it is ruinous as a betrayal of God and as blind idolatry, as blind enslavement by the meaninglessness of worldly life. It is not by chance that the Savior said once and for always, for *all* people and with regard to *all* their works, "Without me ye can do nothing" (John 15:5).

As we have already said, this external activity is not something with which one could genuinely *illuminate one's life with meaning.* And to the extent that such activity pretends to have such a significance, this is always an illusion. Rather, this activity is itself something that is *illuminated with meaning* that has already been found and is being actualized in continuous inner spiritual work; and as such it is necessary and rational in its appropriate form for every human being in his proper place. We can express the same thing from the objective side: all external activity realizes not the goal of life but only a means to this life. This means is rational insofar as we are conscious of a rational goal which it serves, and insofar as we place this means in relation with this goal. And on the contrary, the means is meaningless insofar as it posits itself as the goal of life; in doing so, it does not have the power to realize this pretension and diverts us from service of the true goal.

And this means the following: In our external activity, we legitimately *serve* only that which, *in its own turn, serves* the absolute Proto-source of life, God, and thus the realization of our genuine life. Service of the state is legitimate insofar as the being of the state perceives itself and is perceived by us as service of God, insofar as we understand that this being has its purpose, even if only a relative and subordinate one, in the realization of genuine life. Material cares are legitimate insofar as they serve not the enrichment of life, as a goal in itself or as a means to pleasures and satisfaction, but only the maintenance of life in a measure that is truly necessary given our weakness and that really serves to further our spiritual life (this measure is very small; and therefore riches — which, according to the Savior's words, are an obstacle to the attainment of the Kingdom of Heaven — are harmful). No work or interest, not even natural love for man, which always draws us on by the hope of some higher satisfaction — can be considered the ultimate goal. All this is rational and meaningful insofar as it is a means and a way, insofar as it is *service* — that is, insofar as it serves to assist that inner service which alone is the genuine realization of our life.

And returning to our earlier formulation of the question of the meaning of life, we must recall what we have already learned. When a man gives his life as a means for some particular thing, whatever this particular thing might consist in; when he serves some supposed absolute goal, which does not have any relation to his personal life, to the intimate and fundamental demands of his spirit, to his need to find *himself* in ultimate fulfillment, in the eternal light and peace of perfect fullness — he then inevitably becomes a *slave* and loses the meaning of his life. He attains the meaning of life only when he gives himself to the service of that which is the eternal foundation and source of his personal life. Therefore, all *other* service is justified only to the degree that it indirectly participates in this uniquely genuine service of the Truth, of true life. "And ye shall know the Truth, and the Truth shall make you free" (John 8:32): it will free you from the inevitable slavery in which the idolater lives; and according to the nature of man, everyone is an idolater insofar as he is not illuminated by the Truth.

There does exist one relatively simple criterion according to which it is possible to recognize whether a person has established a correct, internally grounded relation to his external, worldly activity — that is, whether he has grounded this activity upon a connection with his genuine, spiritual work. This is the degree to which this external activity is directed at the most critical needs of the present day, at the vital, concrete needs of the people around us. One who has wholly devoted himself to work for the sake of the remote future, for the well-being of distant strangers, for homeland, mankind, future generations, and so on; who is indifferent, inattentive, and neglectful in relation to the people around him; who considers his concrete obligations toward these people, the needs of the present day, something inessential and insignificant compared with the great importance of the work that occupies him — this person is unquestionably an idolater. One who speaks of his great historical mission and of the expected radiant future and does not consider it necessary to warm and illuminate the present day, to make it even a little more rational and meaningful for himself and for his neighbors — this person, if he is not a hypocrite, is an idolater. And conversely, the more concrete a person's moral activity is, the more it takes into account the concrete needs of living human beings and is concentrated on the present day — in other words, the more it is permeated not with abstract principles but with the living sense of love or the living consciousness of the obligation to lovingly assist other people — the closer this person will be to subordinating his external activity to the spiritual task of his life. The commandment not to concern oneself with tomorrow, for "sufficient unto the day is the evil thereof" (Matt. 6:34), is not only a commandment not to overburden oneself with excessive earthly cares, but also the demand to limit oneself to the cares of real life, and not to the objects of dreams and abstract thought. *Today* I live and the people around me live; *today* is a matter of will and life. *Tomorrow* is the domain of dreams and abstract possibilities. *Tomorrow* it is easy to accomplish the greatest exploits, to make the life of the whole world better, to institute a rational life. *Today, now* — it is difficult to defeat and destroy one's weakness; it is difficult to devote to the poor man and the sick man a moment of attention, to help them even a little; it is difficult to force oneself to accomplish even a small moral work.

But precisely this small work, this self-overcoming even if only in small things, this manifestation, even if tiny, of active love for people, is my obligation, the direct expression and verification of the degree to which my life is genuinely illuminated with meaning. This is because the work of the present day and hour, and my relations with my neighbor, are directly connected with the concreteness of my life, with the eternal substance of the latter. Directing myself at the eternal, striving to fulfill God's commandments and to nourish myself from the eternal source of life, I must necessarily realize the closest concrete works in which the eternal principle of life finds its expression. One who lives in the present day without giving himself to it but rather subordinating it to himself — this person lives in eternity. This right attitude finds its moral-psychological expression in humility, in the consciousness of the limitedness of one's powers, and also in the *tranquility* and *stability* of soul with which are accomplished these works of the present day, this participation in the concrete life of the world; whereas idolatrous service of the world is, on the one hand, always manifested in pride and frenzy and, on the other hand, is connected with a sense of agitation, uncertainty, and vanity. This is because one who sees as the fundamental goal of his activity the attainment of some specific external result, the realization of an objective change in the structure of the world — this person, on the one hand, must exaggerate the significance of his work as well as his own powers; and on the other hand, owing to the instability and blindness inherent in the course of all earthly works, he will never be certain of success and will therefore place his life in dependence on conditions over which his will has no power. Only one who lives in the eternal and considers the task of his activity to be the maximally possible active manifestation of eternal forces irrespective of their external success and objective result; only one who lives in the consciousness expressed by the French saying *"Fais ce que dois, advienne que pourra"*[7] — only this person lives in repose of soul and, in his external work, is not torn from the inner roots of his being, from his fundamental inner work, directed at the strengthening of these roots.

---

7. "Do your duty, come what may." *Trans.*

Thus, external, worldly work — since it is derivative of fundamental, spiritual work and is made meaningful only by the latter — must be put in its proper place in our general spiritual life if it is not to disrupt the normal spiritual equilibrium. Forces of the spirit, strengthened and nourished from inside, must freely pour outward, for faith without works is dead; the light coming from the depths must illuminate the outer darkness. But the forces of the spirit must not serve and become subject to the meaningless forces of the world; the darkness must not overwhelm the eternal Light.

This is, after all, that living Light "which lighteth every man that cometh into the world" (John 1:9). This is the God-Man Christ Himself, who is for us "the way, the truth, and the life" (John 14:6), and who precisely for this reason is the eternal and inviolable *meaning of our life.*

The Spiritual Emptiness of Our Time and the Meeting with the Living God*

> *Tormented by spiritual thirst,*
> *I dragged myself through a somber desert.*[1]

What follows from all this? Or rather (since we are not concerned here with arguments and theories), where have we arrived?[2] What remains in our possession, and how are we to live?

All the idols which we had served enthusiastically and the service of which gave meaning to our lives — all these idols have lost their enchantment and cannot attract our souls, no matter how many people around us continue to worship them. All we have left is the thirst for life — for full, living, and profound life. All we have left is certain ultimate and profound demands and desires of our spirit, which we do not know how to satisfy or even how to express.

---

1. These lines are from Pushkin's poem "The Prophet." *Trans.*

2. Here, Frank is preparing to draw conclusions from the previous chapters of *The Fall of the Idols* concerning the collapse of a number of "idols" sacred to nineteenth-century intellectuals: the idol of the revolution, the idol of politics, the idol of culture, and the idol of "moral idealism." *Trans.*

---

*This is the concluding chapter of Frank's book *The Fall of the Idols*. For a discussion of this book, see the Translator's Foreword. *Trans.*

For the negative result of our survey of spiritual wanderings[3] can by no means satisfy us. There was once an epoch in our spiritual past when this negative result could have appeared to be a great positive revelation for many of us. This is perhaps the last idol, and the most imperfect and lifeless one, which our soul encounters on these pathways. This idol is the phantom of total personal freedom. We have already encountered this idol and have pointed out that, compared with the tyranny of moral norms, it tempts us with the hint at some sort of life truth. But this temptation is brief and is easily exposed as falsehood; only the most naïve and inexperienced souls can, for a time, succumb to it. To seek nothing, to serve nothing, to enjoy life, to take from it all that it has to give, to satisfy every desire, every passion, to be powerful and daring, to lord over life — at times this seems alluring; and, as we have indicated, there was once a brief epoch — it can be called the epoch of Nietzsche — when many considered this to be the highest life-wisdom.

There is no need for us here to refute this pseudo-wisdom with abstract arguments. I think that most of us have changed since that epoch, and that this temptation has no effect upon us. Freedom from all things in the world — why do we need such freedom if we do not know for what purpose we are free? Will freedom give us much? Are all the pleasures and intoxications produced by the simple unleashing of the elemental desires really that great? Our souls have aged, and we regard skeptically not only so-called ideals but also all the so-called pleasures of life. We know very well that every moment of happiness is purchased at the cost of suffering or the anguish of repletion. We know that there is immeasurably more grief in life than happiness and joy; we have known poverty; we clearly see the inevitable end of all life — death, in the face of which all things become equally illusory. In a word, our sense of *the meaninglessness of life* is too acute to permit us to be captivated by the naked process of life. And the word *freedom* in this sense even seems to us insultingly inappropriate. Is that man free who, without meaning or goal, stumbles from side to side, wandering on no road, spurred on only by the desires of the present minute, desires whose meaninglessness he is well

---

3. That is, the negative result Frank arrived at in the previous chapters of *The Fall of the Idols. Trans.*

aware of? Is that man free who does not know how to escape spiritual idleness and spiritual poverty? In the face of such "temptations," one recalls with anguish the dumb old joke, but in this case full of symbolic meaning: "Cabbie, are you free?" "Yes, I'm free." "Well, then, shout: 'Long live freedom!'"

Joyous intoxication by life which surpasses the usual bounds and usual order of things, genuine — always temporary — rapture from the unleashing of passions, a rapture resulting not from despair but from an excess of the soul's powers — such an intoxication and rapture are apparently possible only when, in the depths of the soul, there lives a belief in some sort of ultimate stability and inviolability of life. Just as a small child is mischievously and even wildly playful when he finds himself in the calm refuge of his own home and can rely on the unshakable stability of his parents' authority, but becomes unchildishly serious and quiet in a foreign environment, when his soul is full of alarm and uncertainty — so, in the same way, all of us, experiencing the shaking of the spiritual ground beneath our feet, have lost the capacity for childlike lightheartedness, for the boldness of wild merriment — for that which the Germans call *Ubermut,* a beautiful but untranslatable word. In order to delight in joyful intoxication, it is necessary to have one's own home and to be assured that one can peacefully regain sobriety there. Otherwise, only the wild revelry of despair is possible — that bitter, heavy drunkenness to which Marmeladov[4] devotes himself, because he has "no place to go."

That which we seek and long for is not freedom but stability, not chaotic wandering over infinite distances but peace in one's own home. We are thrown from side to side by the turbulent waves of life; and we dream of putting our foot down on unshakably solid ground. Or, more correctly, we hang in the air above an abyss, for we have lost the inner connection of our spirit, of our personality, with being, and we desire to restore this connection, to find support on solid spiritual ground. We suffer not from an excess but from a lack of spiritual strength. We have lost our strength and grown weary in the desert; our soul seeks not the meaningless expanses of detachment from all things, but, on the contrary, a close and

---

4. Marmeladov is a character in Dostoevsky's *Crime and Punishment. Trans.*

ultimate fusion with something unknown which could, once and for all, fill, strengthen, and sate it.

Our soul has become impoverished and famished. The loss of faith is not a child's game: The destruction of idols which we and our fathers had worshipped for so long and so passionately is not an easy thing. It is probable that our ancestors, the ancient Slavs, experienced a similar fear, emptiness, and anguish when Perun together with the other idols was cast into the Dnieper; and they too did not know whom they should serve and whom they should ask for help in their troubles.[5] For renunciation of idols is not a betrayal, not a rejection of faith and a fall into iniquitous dishonesty; rather, it indicates a change of faith, and even if the new faith has not yet been found, the fall of the old faith is nonetheless already a sign of a passionate search and agonizing longing for the new faith.

Fortunate is he who, in this anguish, in these torments of spiritual hunger and thirst, has a dear soul close to him — be it friend, mother, or wife — to whom he can pour out his anguish or in whose presence he can at least find a moment of repose from his anguish. For it often happens that we can fully convey what torments us neither to the people most dear to us nor even to ourselves. And woe to him who is alone!

But all of us do have a being kindred and close to us: our homeland. The more unfortunate we are, the emptier our souls — the more fervently we love her and long for her. If nowhere else, then at least here, we feel clearly that our homeland is not an "idol," and that our love for her is not an infatuation with a phantom. Our homeland is a real, living being. We love her, after all, not by virtue of the "principle of patriotism"; we do not worship her glory or her power, or any other abstract traits and principles of her being. We love her for herself, our ancient, primordial mother; she is now unfortunate, dishonored, sick with a dangerous ailment, deprived of all grandeur, of all visible dignities and virtues; she is also spiritually sick, together with all of us, her children.[6] We can love her

5. Perun was the chief god in pre-Christian Kievan Russia. After the conversion of Russia to Christianity at the end of the tenth century, Prince Vladimir the Great ordered the statue of Perun which stood on a hill in Kiev to be cast into the Dnieper River. *Trans.*

6. Frank is referring to the destruction of old Russia by the Revolution and the institution of the Soviet regime. His point of view here is that of the Russian exiles, longing to return to their homeland. *Trans.*

now only with that "strange love" which was confessed by the great anguished Russian poet, so close to us, the poet who was "a wanderer with a Russian soul chased by the world."[7]

At the present time, this "strange love" is for us the only genuine, simple love — an all-forgiving, all-consuming love. In the frenzy of political passions, which most of us do not really believe in anymore but rouse in ourselves in order to fill our spiritual emptiness, and to which, nearly a hundred years ago, that very same poet referred so bitterly ("and there reigns in the soul some sort of secret coldness,/when a fire burns in the blood"[8]) — in this fog of frenzy, we often forget our genuine love and involuntarily renounce our unfortunate mother, the sole treasure that we have left on earth.

We like to make a show of her shame; with malicious joy, we find comfort in her suffering; we even like to exaggerate her sorrow and the depths of her moral fallenness, because we cannot reconcile ourselves with the false path our homeland has taken. We shift to others and to our homeland herself the responsibility for her sins and misfortunes which lies equally upon all of us, her children. We are often ready to identify her soul, so dear and kindred to us — her soul which is (we know this) everlasting — with the violent and abominable deeds of her vicious children, the violators, who now mock her. But all this is taking place in the superficial stratum of our souls. What we truly feel about our homeland is expressed not in words, not in conscious arguments and judgments, but in that anguished longing, in those tears of tenderness with which we think about our native meadows and forests, about our native customs, with which we listen to the sounds of our native songs. We then know that there is nothing dearer and more beautiful in the world than our homeland.

> Give your dangerous beauty
> To whatever sorcerer you wish.
> Let him bewitch and betray you,
> But you will not perish, not vanish.

7. The poet is Mikhail Lermontov, and the line is from his poem "Homeland." *Trans.*
8. These lines are from Lermontov's poem "A Thought." *Trans.*

Yes, care will cloud
Your beautiful features,
But you will remain the same — woods and meadows,
And a patterned kerchief
Down to your eyebrows.[9]

If only we could help our homeland to rise from the dead, to be renewed, to appear to the world in all her beauty and spiritual power — we
then might be able to find (or so it seems to us) a way out for our anguished longing, even if we had to give up our lives for this! But precisely
here we feel the hopelessness of our situation, of our dream. And this is
not at all because the "Bolsheviks are still in power," because we do not
know how to overthrow them and cannot see the end of their reign. Anyone who still believes that the salvation of our homeland will consist in a
simple "overthrow of the Bolsheviks," that the "Bolsheviks" are some sort
of external and accidental evil whose external removal will re-institute
the reign of truth and happiness in Russia — anyone who still lives by a
belief in this political idol, who is still intoxicated by this revolutionary
narcotic with an inverse composition — this person is not familiar with
our anguished longing, and it is not for him that these lines are being
written. But, unfortunately, we know very well that it is impossible to
help anyone, including our homeland, if we ourselves are helpless, that a
pauper cannot enrich anyone, and that a sick man cannot become anyone's healer. We know that we have the same sickness as our homeland,
however different the symptoms might be, and that we can only be
healed together with our homeland — if we are healed at all! We will direct our homeland to a new and true path only when we find this path
for ourselves.

Thus, just as we are not saved by our love for those dear to us (this
love only moderates but does not put an end to our spiritual anguish), so
we are not saved by the most sincere, the most fervent, the most selfless
love for our homeland. The very faith in our homeland, without which
love for her is inconceivable, is rooted (as we clearly feel) in some other,
more profound, and more all-embracing faith, in which we are not yet es-

9. This excerpt is from Alexander Blok's poem "Russia." *Trans.*

tablished, which we have yet to find in our souls with irrefutable and unshakable self-evidence. Although, in itself, love does not require any foundation or grounding, without this faith it is nonetheless deprived of some ultimate stability, of some profound justification. It is certain that many nations have perished from external misfortunes or from spiritual degeneration. How are we, Russians, better than the others, and why do we think that, in this global earthquake, we can keep from disappearing? Perhaps Russia is as much a mirage as everything else that surrounds us. In our spiritual emptiness, we cannot find a convincing refutation of this nightmarish fantasy.

No, we feel this with certainty: Without a faith in something primordial, fundamental, unshakable; without some ultimate, profound foundation on which our spirit could be grounded — no earthly attractions or fascinations, no love or attachment, can save us. On these pathways, in this hopeless wandering with no way out in this boundless and trackless desert, when our anguish and spiritual thirst reach their extreme and become intolerable — it is then that the meeting of the soul with the living God occurs.

This inexpressible meeting occurs differently for everyone who experiences it. It can suddenly shake the soul; or it can be prepared in the soul by a slow process of illumination. The existence of such a meeting cannot be proved in a "universally obligatory" manner to anyone who has not experienced it, whose soul has not been prepared for it. In itself, it cannot even be described. But it is nevertheless possible to talk about the general features of this meeting; it is possible to tell about those forces of the soul which push one toward it; and mainly, it is possible to tell about the great consequences of this experience for the fate of the soul.

Perhaps the easiest way to explain how and why this meeting occurs is to attempt to clarify for ourselves *what* it is we are seeking, what it is we need, and what it is we are anguished by. We sense in ourselves the presence of certain indestructible and powerful spiritual desires which remain unsatisfied. What do these desires consist of? What is it we need? It is not correct to say that we are seeking something "holy" which we could worship, that we are seeking authentic "ideals" which we could serve. Such elevated words have for us a cold and unconvincing sound;

and after all our experience, we regard them with suspicion. For us, in our present state, there is something inauthentic in these words, some falseness which offends the ear: they remind us of that windbag in Ostrovsky's play who liked to repeat, "All is sublime, all is beautiful, Anfisa Pavlovna. . . ."[10]

On the contrary, that which we seek is something very real and simple — even something crude and non-ideal but, for all that, authentic. We seek real life, life's fullness and stability. It is in general not clear to us whether we should serve someone or something; and in any case we do not know what we must serve. But that we want to and must *live* — this we understand sufficiently well and do not need to prove. But nevertheless *we do not live;* the sources of life are drying up; the supplies of nourishment which until now had sustained our lives have run out or are running out; we are barely saving ourselves from a hungry death by dry crusts of bread left over from the past. We are perishing. And for this reason we are not seeking any "service," any "ideals," any morality; we are only seeking salvation, personal salvation. Let the moralists view this as nothing more than egotism; let them preach to us whatever they like, but we know that this profound thirst for self-preservation does not need any justification, for it has ultimate certainty for us — it is the one thing that matters. We know that a drowning man has the right to demand help and that, when we see him, we should not begin to expound on the service of ideals. We should simply pull him out of the water.

We are drowning because the ground on which we tried to stand was actually quicksand, and sucked us in; but we are seeking solid ground beneath our feet. We cannot ground ourselves upon any "ideals," because they have turned out to be phantoms. Instead of sustaining our spirit, these "ideals" take it prisoner and demand from us self-sacrifice, the diminution and perversion of our life, in their name. Nor can we ground ourselves upon ourselves, solely upon the thirst for life or the inner force of life in us, for this is to hang in air. No, we need authentic ground: a spiritual reality which would be something other than our

10. This line is from *The Forest* (1871) by the celebrated Russian playwright Alexander Ostrovsky (1823-1886). *Trans.*

own "I" and which thus could support the latter. At the same time, this reality should be something profoundly kindred to our "I"; it should be identical in content to our "I" and thus should not take anything away from it, should not be hostile to it, but should give it everything and help it in all things. We have to cling close to someone; we have to take hold of someone's powerful and beneficent hand, and hold it for always. We will be saved not by an "ideal," not by moral judgments, and not by words and arguments.

We can be saved only by love — but by the love of such a being and for such a being that would not be so weak, powerless, and poor as we are, that would stand firmly on its feet and would be rich enough to feed and give drink to our spirit. We are powerless children who are lost in a strange land and who seek our father or mother. Our spirit has been torn away from its roots and is fading; and it is convulsively seeking to be re-united with these roots and to plunge deep into the primordial maternal womb of its native soil, in order to blossom once again and to begin to bring forth fruit. If we are to stop feeling a deathly emptiness in our depths, in the final end of our spirit, so to speak, it is necessary that our spirit not have this end; it is necessary that it be directly connected with the infinite spirit. If our life is not to dry up, it is necessary that it be nourished from within by the eternal source of life.

In order to find what you are seeking, all you have to do is to understand completely the meaning and object of your seekings. And here there can easily happen to us what happened to the contemporary English writer Chesterton, as he relates with good-natured irony: "All of my life I sought the truth and thought that nobody knew it; and I attempted to be at least several years ahead of my century. But one fine day I understood that I had fallen exactly nineteen centuries behind the truth."[11]

After all, it is true that the truth was proclaimed to the world nineteen centuries ago. It was the Living Truth itself that was revealed to the world then, and to men there was revealed exactly what we are now seeking so excruciatingly and, apparently, so hopelessly. We have grown weary of all arguments and ideas; we have stopped believing in them and

---

11. This is a back-translation from the Russian. *Trans.*

have become spiritually impoverished. But Christ said, "Blessed are the poor in spirit: for theirs is the kingdom of heaven" (Matt. 5:3). We seek not a moral judgment, but simply salvation from spiritual death. He also said, "I came not to judge the world, but to save the world" (John 12:47). We thirst for a love which could sustain us, and He proclaimed that God is love, that we have a Father, an eternal and all-powerful Father who loves His children and will not refuse anything to one who asks. We seek a truth which could spiritually illuminate us. We seek the true path in life, which would not destroy our life but would be an expression of the true, most profound power of life, concealed in us and, excruciatingly, finding no way out for itself. He also said, "I am the way, the truth, and the life" (John 14:6) — and in these three words He expressed and gave to us that inexpressible, authentic, ultimate thing which we seek. We are made weary by both the heaviness and the emptiness of life, and His response is, "Come unto me, all ye that labor and are heavy laden, and I will give you rest" (Matt. 11:28). We seek a service that would not kill our souls and that would give us joy and peace, and He gives us an easy yoke and a light burden (Matt. 11:30).

It is astonishing how these old, familiar words, which we are accustomed to hearing since childhood and which precisely for that reason usually do not have any particular meaning for us — it is astonishing how these words respond — with a precise, simple, and superhuman meaning — to our need and contain precisely what we are asking for and what we ourselves are often not able to express, not only to others, but even to ourselves. Anyone who has once experienced this with ultimate clarity, with a power corresponding to the significance of its content; anyone who has received it into himself in the same way that — confronted by insuperable calamity and already considering himself lost — he hears the voice of a friend, encouraging him and proclaiming his salvation; anyone who has received into himself this image of God who knows the totality of our human need, of God who took upon Himself all the sins and sufferings of the world — this person will no longer be perplexed by any doubts; he will find simply uninteresting all abstract, spiritually blind philosophical argumentation about religion, all historical conjectures about the "true" person of Christ, or about the origin of belief in Christ. If we ever met a man who, with full and ultimate clarity, could reveal to us our own soul; a man who, without questioning us about anything, could explain to us everything in our soul that is incomprehensible even to us; a man who could find words of consolation and healing, giving us exactly what we need — we would know with perfect certainty that we have a true friend and mentor, infinitely rich in spirit. And if he did this not by words alone, but with his whole life, with his whole being, manifesting to the world in his person the incarnation of the supreme and absolute truth, in such a way that this truth, once expressed and revealed in all its fullness in a living human being, would live in our own soul as the eternal principle of the latter, as the unshakable support and inexhaustible source of life — we would know with certainty that our mentor and savior is the Divine and Eternal Spirit Himself, that He is always with us, that He did not die and cannot die. *And we know this.*

Now, after this has been revealed to us, we understand the meaning of our seekings, of our anguished longing. We seek salvation; we seek true and eternal life, that ultimate, most profound source of life, which at the same time is light, joy, and peace. As Augustine said, How could we seek Him if we did not already have Him? For a seeking that does not find satisfaction in any goods or values of the world presupposes a dim seeing of something other — of perfect, all-embracing, and eternal life. But where could such a seeking in our spirit come from if our spirit had a wholly earthly, worldly origin, if beyond the sensuously known there were for us nothing else, no mysterious, transcendent depths? What is the force that chases us from one aspiration to another, not permitting us to be content with any one of them? What is it that compels us to renounce the idols and expose their emptiness and evil? What is it that pounds in us with unstoppable waves, ripping apart all chains and inundating all limited forms, all the shores with which earthly life constrains us? Where does this force in us come from? Where does this absurd faith in the limitlessness and supreme value of our spirit come from if our spirit is only a small, impotent, human soul, a product of heredity, environment, and education?

If we are able to "to turn the eyes of the soul," as Plato said; if we are able to look attentively into our own soul and see *our own anguished longing and dissatisfaction* as a manifestation of a new and *profound on-*

tological reality in the ultimate recesses of our own spirit — we will become immediately convinced that the object of our seekings is not a phantom, but a genuine reality, not something distant and unattainable, but something infinitely close to us, something that is with us eternally. For the eternal source of life and light which we seek *is precisely that force which compels us to seek it* in the first place. About these confused, obscure, impotent seekings, one can say the same thing that the great mystics knew and expressed about prayer: they knew that prayer itself is grace sent by God, that God hears us before we address Him, and that He Himself draws us to call to Him. In these seekings it is revealed that, in our soul, there already lives — in an obscure and unknown manner for us — the image of the true God as the God of life, the God of truth and love. We sense an emptiness in the depths of our soul; it is as if the inner end of our spirit has been torn away and, like the exposed end of a nerve, reacts with excruciating pain to all external touches. But why is this so? It is because we know that our spirit must sit firmly with its roots deep in the spiritual soil; and thus we know or foresee that this soil, this infinite reality of spiritual life, *exists.* And at the same moment when we have consciously understood that we know this — at this moment and in virtue of this knowledge, we are experiencing a *real* contact with spiritual life; we are already living in and with this life.

Now we can also clearly understand why all the idols that we worshipped *had to fall,* and what their fall signifies. The fall of the idols is excruciating for us; we experience it as if it were a devastation of our soul, the death of all the life forces and impulses of our soul. But, in fact, we now see that the fall of the idols is actually a liberation, the purging of illusory and dead simulacra of life from our soul. We see that it is a purification that is absolutely necessary if our soul is to be immersed in the eternal and all-embracing source of *authentic life,* a purification already being accomplished in us by waters of this source which, without our knowing it, have entered our soul. All our dreams directed at the future and the willfully human creation of the future, all the "ideals" and "norms" which, as such, we ourselves *oppose* to reality — all these things are phantoms, shadows, and false simulacra of being, deprived of roots in That Which Exists, in true life. That which truly exists is not a dream that is born out of nothing in the solitary human soul and has yet to be actualized in the future; nor — paraphrasing Hegel's words — is that which truly exists merely an "idea" which does not exist but only "should exist." That which exists is true, infinitely full, eternal Being; it is living infinite life and the authentically real, all-powerful, creative power of love. That which exists creates new life; it perfects us and the whole world not out of poverty, not out of the emptiness of non-being, longing to be filled, but out of an infinite excess of reality, pouring forth on all the frail sprouts of being and compelling them to flower and bear fruit. Nor is that which exists a dead schema, a formula pretending to be life, an abstractly processed part of the living flesh of being, a part which desires to supplant being and which therefore fatally engenders only death and hatred, which destroy all living things. That which exists, being true life, is infinite love which heals all the ailments of our limited being, all of the defects of this being, and which even raises the dead, summoning and impelling all that is dead to submerge itself in the living water and to be reborn in it, to come to life.

In the end, only that perished which should have perished, and it perished because it did not have any life within itself, but was only a dead and illusory simulacrum of life, luring us with a mirage and a will-o'-the-wisp. In the fact that it perished there is no longer anything frightening for us which could cause us to despair. And in general there is no longer anything that could cause us to despair. Descending down into the depths of our devastated spirit, we have finally reached solid and unshakable ground, on which we can stand firmly with both feet. Through the infinite darkness, a light has shined for us, which from now on will inwardly illuminate us.

At the first moment, this meeting with God, this sensation of solid ground beneath our feet and the discovery of the inner light, does not change anything for us in everything else, in the external world, in our relations with other people and with earthly life. What has happened is that we have found in our soul a source of inexhaustible joy, a sense of stability and peace. We have found the eternal Friend and Father; we are no longer alone and abandoned; in tranquility, alone with ourselves and with God, we are delighting in the joy of love, compared with which all the failures, disappointments, and woes of external life are inessential and insignificant.

... Amidst our random vanities,
Within the turbid stream of life's anxieties
You possess a wholly joyous secret:
Evil is powerless. We are eternal. God is with us.[12]

Now when we listen to the usual conversations, when we hear about the usual interests, passions, and humdrum concerns of human life, a good-humoredly ironic smile comes to our lips — the smile of a person who knows a great secret which has wholly changed his life and given it a new meaning and direction. We know that people think that they are poor; they are preoccupied with arduous cares, with a somber, wearying, and embittering struggle for existence; and they do not know that they possess an enormous inheritance, an immense fortune, which will assure them a joyous and peaceful life forever. But *we do know* about this treasure; we have already stumbled upon it and therefore understand very well how laughable and empty their cares and worries are.

This inner treasure, this gift of immense love, initially only opposes, as inner being and an inner possession, the entirety of external life and the external environment. Moreover, this inner light is often so blindingly bright that everything else grows dim before it. Everything appears to us inessential, uninteresting, insignificant compared with our inner riches. Perhaps we resemble people who are egotistically in love and who, for the sake of the happiness of their love, forget everything else and become indifferent to all other people and to all of life's interests.

But this is only a temporary and transitory disruption of spiritual equilibrium caused by the overwhelming power and intensity of the impression we have received. The event we have experienced leads to a further illumination and development; the power in which we participated must reveal its true creative nature. This event is an inner disclosure of the soul, ending the soul's self-enclosedness, its cold and enfeebled existence in itself. And this power is the power of infinite love, the power of true life. And therefore the soul must continue to disclose itself further; and, gradually, through its primordial connection with God, it will feel the same sort of close inner connection with all human beings and with

12. These lines are from Vladimir Solovyov's poem "Immanuel." *Trans.*

the whole world. And the living revelation of eternal and infinite love as *the ultimate foundation and essence* of our being and of all being must lead to the same thing: through God we gradually learn to love all things insofar as they are a manifestation of authentic being; the power of eternal love, which at first only induced in us love for ourselves, must continue to grow in us and engender love for all things and all beings. The *Philokalia*[13] has a beautiful metaphor attributed to Abba Dorotheus: If we imagine that people are moving along the radii of a circle, the closer they come to the center of the circle — the absolute center of being and life, God — the closer they come to one another. There is also another metaphor, which is mentioned by numerous religiously illuminated thinkers: just as the leaves of a tree are separated and as if isolated from one another, but in reality live and turn green only by virtue of the juices that flow through them from one common trunk and root, and are nourished by the moisture of a common soil — so human beings too, outwardly isolated and closed off from one another, are inwardly — through their common connection with the all-embracing Source of life — fused together in one integral life.

Thus, instead of a variety of "ideals," principles, and norms, luring our soul onto false paths, leading it into a dead end, and making it weary, we now come upon two commandments, which are sufficient for illuminating our life with meaning, for enriching, strengthening, and quickening it: the commandment of an immeasurable, infinite love for God as the Source of love and of life; and the commandment of love for people, growing out of the sense of the all-unity of human life rooted in God, out of the consciousness of brotherhood based on our common filial relation to the Father. And these two commandments are expressed, and were expressed, as one: we are commanded to strive for perfection, to strive (to the extent we are able) to become like our Heavenly Father as the Perfect Source of love and life. And these two commandments (or one commandment) do not appear to us from outside, with the cold and incomprehensible authority of moral "norms" or prescriptions. Rather, we understand them inwardly, as the necessary ways of our salvation, of the

---

13. The *Philokalia* is a compendium of Eastern Orthodox spiritual and ascetic writings. *Trans.*

preservation of our life. We are judged not like criminals, upon whom an indifferent judge passes sentence in the name of a cold juridical law which is ignorant of the intimate needs of our soul. Rather, we are judged by the voice of our Father, who loves us and guides us to the path of salvation; from this inner judgment we learn which path leads us to life and which path leads us to death; we learn where our salvation lies, and where our perdition.

And much that had previously seemed to us to be a dead idol and really was exposed by us as an idol is now — in a different form and with a totally different meaning — being resurrected in our soul as a living power and as a rational path and rule of life. First of all, this pertains to the whole domain of morality. We did not understand why we were obligated to break and cripple our life for the sake of certain abstract principles; and our spirit, thirsting for freedom and life, protested against such compulsion. And, in fact, we became sufficiently convinced that the areligious morality of principles, the morality of duty and of the categorical imperative, is an idol which does not improve life but only destroys it. But now we discover in ourselves a new living source of morality that is meaningful and comprehensible to us. Inwardly, we can now answer the question why we are obligated to do things we do not want to do, why we must suppress in ourselves the natural desires of our soul. We can cite the example of a sick man, who, in order to be cured, must take bitter medications and suppress the most powerful desires of his body; or the example of a drowning man, who, in order to find his way ashore and thus save his own life, must exert all of his strength, must — however difficult it might be — keep his head above water and swim not with the current that will carry him into the abyss, but against the current.

We understand very well that all morality is nothing else but such a hygiene or *technique* for the salvation, or preservation, of one's life; it consists in self-evidently rational rules for the protection of that "treasure in heaven" which is the sole source and the sole means of our existence and about which we so often forget in our natural blindness and thoughtlessness. This task — the task of not losing the treasure once it has been found, of not being separated from it again, of not burying one's talent in the ground but of allowing it to grow and using its benefits — this task is not always easy for us: it demands constant vigilance from us, a struggle with our blind desires, a courageous power of the will, a severe stubbornness. Nevertheless, this task is a joyous and meaningful work, which is immediately rewarded a hundred times over and which therefore, despite all its difficulty, is easy to accomplish.

In the light of the knowledge of true being that we have gained, we gradually discover or, at least, make out the contours of a whole new world — the sphere of *the spiritual foundations* of life. And this world is ruled by strict, inexorable laws, which are not less exact (although of a different order) than those that govern the physical world. This is what the great Christian thinker Pascal called *l'ordre du coeur* or *la logique du coeur* — the "order" or "logic" of the human heart. The fundamental traits of this order are indicated by the precepts of Christianity; these traits are revealed in Christianity, which is the absolute truth of the human soul. It is precisely in this sense that one should understand Tertullian's subtle statement that "the soul is, by nature, a Christian." This "order of the heart" cannot be violated with impunity, for it is the condition of the meaningfulness and stability of our life, the condition of our spiritual equilibrium and thus of our very being. One can violate the order of the heart with impunity no more than one can violate with impunity the laws of bodily health, the normal order of organic life, or the laws of mechanics and physics.

This spiritual order of being, which is "unto the Jews a stumbling block, and unto the Greeks foolishness" (1 Cor. 1:23), that is, something that appears to be inadmissible for those who know only the external norms and political ideals of life, and something that appears to be meaningless for those who know only the life of the natural world — this spiritual order of being is, for one who sees, the strict absolute truth, which grounds his entire life and assures its higher rationality. Being abstractly unprovable, morality as a self-sufficient knowledge derives — with total necessity, with the complete predetermination of its structure — from the religious understanding of the world. Being a living, humane morality of love and salvation, it is also a strict morality of asceticism, of self-limitation and self-sacrifice, for its fundamental law precisely proclaims that it is impossible to save one's soul without losing it, and that it is impossible to acquire the Kingdom of Heaven except by carrying one's cross. For "wide is the gate, and broad is the way, that leadeth to destruction . . . [and] . . . strait is the gate, and narrow is the way, which leadeth unto life" (Matt. 7:13-14). And we now understand the ruinous falsehood of amoralism, which grants man the freedom to perish and feeds sweets to the sick soul, whereas, in order to be cured, the soul needs bitter medicine. We even understand the relative value of the usual unilluminated, *heteronomous* (*contra* Kant) morality, for until man reaches a state of enlightenment, he needs certain external rules, which restrain his willfulness and protect him against evil, however inevitably imperfect these means might be and however frequently they might be taken for self-sufficient higher principles and thus degenerate into evil.

All the same, this living religious morality is profoundly different in its inner structure from the dead morality of duty and the "moral ideal." For this religious morality is permeated with a living sense of the presence of the real source of life and also with the consciousness of the imperfection and weakness of man's nature. And this morality is wholly a radiance of love, a striving for salvation. Therefore, in this morality, hatred for evil never degenerates into hatred for the very essence of life and for concrete human beings. Religious asceticism is a beneficent asceticism of salvation, not the cruel and frenzied asceticism of moral fanaticism. Here, a man attempts to be pitilessly strict with *himself,* for he desires to be truly reborn and is afraid of losing the great treasure that has been entrusted to him. But, conscious of his own sinfulness, he will not judge others harshly, and he will attempt to be not their judge, but their helper. For he lives not by the morality of judgment, but by the morality of salvation; and he knows very well that, on the one hand, all human beings are equally undeserving of the great gifts of grace given to them by God and that, on the other hand, they are all children of God, who will not be abandoned by their Father. For one who truly believes, it is impossible to conceive of the hypocritical and fatal division of life into two types of moral life: one which is official and for show, and one which is intimate and authentic. For it is a question of personal salvation, of the satisfaction of the profoundest and truest need of the soul; and there is no impoverishment and withering of the soul here, but rather its immeasurable enrichment and blossoming. Here, the process of being made perfect is a great personal happiness, which, in embarrassment, tends to hide from people in the deep recesses of the soul, rather than brazenly attract attention to itself. And through all this there wafts the spirit of love, as the very essence of life and salvation. Thus, here it is impossible to conceive of the cold severity of external moral struggle, inimical to and alienated from the living human soul. Instead, what we have here is loving help in the awakening of true light in the souls of brothers. Here it is immediately clear that the growth of good is not a mechanical result of the destruction of evil and especially not a mechanical result of the destruction of evil people. Rather, it is the fruit of the organic inner nurturing of good in ourselves and in others. For evil is non-being, emptiness, which pretends to be fullness; it disappears only when it is expelled by the fullness, essentiality, and profound reality of good.

In the same way, in this gracious light, the lost ideals of human relationships and of the universal social organization of men are reborn for us with a new meaning and content. To be sure, we can no longer return to the old idols, and now we have an even better understanding of their falseness: We cannot believe in any absolute order of social organization; nor can we give our allegiance to any political forms or doctrines. We know that the kingdom of true life is not of this world and can never be adequately and fully realized under the conditions of inevitably sinful and imperfect earthly life. But at the same time, we know with full clarity the paths which must be followed by our relations to people and by the evolution of society. We understand, first of all, that the fundamental law of our moral world is the responsibility of all for all, which connects us with the whole world. Conscious of the all-unity of being rooted in God, we clearly see our own responsibility for the evil that reigns in the world, and we just as clearly understand that it is impossible for us to be saved unless all are saved. Just as an individual leaf on a tree cannot turn green when the whole tree is drying up and rotting, since the tree as a whole is unified by a commonality of life — so the social life of men is dominated by an inner solidarity which cannot be violated with impunity. From this flows the fundamental inner rule of love for people and solidarity with them in the name of our own salvation.

But we also know *what* constitutes the true good of human life, and therefore from now on we will not be tempted by any utopias of social paradise, of equality of distribution and universal material well-being. Nor will we be tempted by dreams (inwardly kindred to the utopian dreams, but with an inverse content) of the soulless power of the political state, of earthly grandeur and military glory. We know the true, spiritual foundations and goals of life; and we understand very well that from these foundations and goals there derive both the need for a hierarchy of human life, where the worst are subordinated to the best and all are subordinated to the common law of life, and the need to respect every human person and to treat every person in a brotherly manner. A new instinct of spiritual health and self-preservation — which the wisest among us can develop into a whole system of a hygiene of spiritual being — will from now on guide our entire life: both our personal relations to other people and our attitude toward questions of social life.

When, guided by this immediate sense of living, authentic truth, we survey our present social life and the ideological forces acting in it, we feel that we cannot identify with any of the tendencies dominant in it. To be sure, we reject with disgust the cynical, insolent, and unprincipled disbelief with which the ruling powers in Russia today are trampling upon and mocking the truth; nor can we make the slightest spiritual concession to this disbelief and take the position of spiritual compromise which comes from a double desire — to defend oneself against pure evil and, at the same time, to keep in step with the "spirit of the time" in which this evil and insanity are the dominant power. On the other hand, we must also reject all those who, either from a sincere impulse or from pharisaical pride, are turning their purity into filth by surrounding themselves with a wall of hatred for all that is essential; all those who, with morbid exaltation, are devoting themselves to a fanatical cult of sociopolitical idols overthrown long ago; all those who, as in the past (but now with an inverse content), are confusing religious faith with abstract morality, and morality with political "principles."

For us, the spiritual universe does not fit into the linear dimension of right to left; and the cult of the "right" is, for us, the same sort of idolatry as the cult of the "left." In the midst of the whirlpool which has captured us, when the old, habitual forms of life are collapsing and some new, hitherto unknown life is ripening, and when, at the same time, the strength of the human spirit is being tested — we are conscious of the need to strictly distinguish the eternal from the temporal, the absolute from the relative. The strangeness of our life, its instability and fluidity, the newness of the conditions of our life, demand from us that we combine an unshakably firm devotion to the eternal principles, which are being subjected to mockery and doubt, with spiritual breadth and freedom, with a sensitive, unprejudiced relation to the real nature of life and its needs. This combination of firm fidelity to the truth with total spiritual freedom, with the readiness for martyrdom in the name of the truth, with tolerance toward people, with the readiness to come into living contact with them in the midst of the evil reigning in the world without fearing that we will be polluted — this combination is given only to the religious spirit, to the spirit which has attained the living eternal truth and is illuminated by its gracious spirit. Our attitude toward unbelievers and toward idolaters is both one of rejection and one of tolerant love for the wayward human soul; and we go our own way.

And — to finish this inexhaustible list of spiritual riches — we find now a right relation not only to other individuals and to social orders and tendencies, but also to collective, supra-individual living organisms. That which, previously, we had, at best, only an obscure sense of, we now understand and see: that is, we understand and see that these supra-individual wholes are living spiritual entities which have their own value and the fate of which also determines our personal fate. By overcoming the inner self-enclosedness of our soul, by opening our soul and allowing it to participate in the all-one living foundation of being, we immediately participate inwardly also in the supratemporal all-unity of people, living, like us, in God and with God — we participate in the supra-individual soul of the church as the unity of holiness and religious life, as the eternal keeper of holy truths and traditions. From the perception of eternal being and our living nearness to Divinity there immediately flows the perception of the church as the living universal soul of humankind, as a collective personality through the connection with which we participate in the universal, cosmic sacrament of communion with God. The church is the true maternal womb of our entire spiritual life.

Furthermore, in the fullness of our concrete earthly life, we participate in the supra-individual soul of our homeland; we not only feel obscurely but now meaningfully understand our homeland as a living entity, as our mother; and we know the connection of our life with her life, the interdependence of our salvation and hers. We understand that our homeland — just as the whole world, just as we ourselves — is perishing from blindness, from winds of malice and hatred swirling in the world; we understand that the salvation from this perdition consists not in any political fanaticism, but only in spiritual rebirth, in the growth of an inwardly meaningful, love-filled relation to life. We are no longer shifting the responsibility for this onto those whom we consider our political enemies; and we no longer boast of our own civic virtue. We understand our common sinfulness before our homeland, our share of the blame in her collapse, in the spread of blindness and satanical malice; we are full of love and pity for the concrete, living soul of our nation, fallen now, just as we ourselves are; and we understand how difficult it is for our homeland — and for us together with her — to rise spiritually after this collapse. But together with faith in the living God, which gives us faith in ourselves and in other people, we also acquire a firm faith in our homeland.

We are grateful to God for the path we have followed, however arduous it might have been. The world and our soul had to experience the veneration of the idols as well as the bitterness of gradual disenchantment in them in order to be purified, in order to become liberated and find genuine fullness and spiritual clarity. The great catastrophe that the world is experiencing at the present time is not taking place in vain. This is not just an excruciating period when humanity can do nothing more than mark time; it is not just a meaningless accumulation of purposeless brutalities, abominations, and sufferings. Rather, it is an arduous, purgatorial path for humanity; and perhaps it is not excessively conceited to believe that we, Russians, who have been in the deepest depths of hell and who have tasted, like no one else, all the bitter fruits of the worship of the abomination of Babylon — that we, Russians, will be the first to pass through this purgatory, and that we will help others to find their way to spiritual resurrection.

Index